ST. JOSEPH
ATLAS
OF THE
BIBLE

TIM DOWLEY

CATHOLIC BOOK PUBLISHING CORP.

Nihil Obstat: Rev. Lawrence E. Frizzell, D.Phil., Censor Librorum
Imprimatur: ✠ Most Rev. John J. Myers, J.C.D., D.D., Archbishop of Newark

Worldwide co-edition produced by Lion
Hudson plc, Wilkinson House, Jordan Hill
Road, Oxford OX2 8DR, England
Tel: + 44 (0) 1865 302750
Fax: + 44 (0) 1865 302757
Email: coed@lionhudson.com.
www.lionhudson.com

Designed by Peter Wyart

Published in the United States in 2007 by
Catholic Book Publishing Corp.
77 West End Road
Totowa, NJ 07512
ISBN: 978-0-89942-655-6
T-655
www.catholicbookpublishing.com

Printed in Singapore

Picture acknowledgments

Photographs

Tim Dowley: pp. 4, 5 top, 6, 8, 9, 12
Top, 13, 22, 28 both, 31 both, 37, 44,
61, 64, 65 reliefs, 68, 72 both, 74
bottom, 78, 79, 80, 82, 83, 87 bottom
Peter Wyart: pp. 1, 5, bottom, 12
bottom, 15, 19, 24, 25, 46, 63, 65
statue, 67, 74 top, 87 top

Illustrations

Richard Scott: pp. 23, 31, 33, 41, 44
James Macdonald: pp. 46, 51, 52, 59,
73.

Maps

Hardlines

CONTENTS

The Lands of the Bible

The story of salvation began to unfold in a particular part of the world and during a particular period of history. It is impossible to understand it without some knowledge of this historical and geographical setting. God disclosed Himself to people living in a certain place at a certain time—in concrete personal situations that are intelligible to every generation. The Biblical record of His dealings with individuals and with the nation of Israel is intended to instruct us (Romans 15:4; 1 Corinthians 10:11).

We need to understand God's ways with people of Bible times, and to know where and when it all happened. A study of the land and story of the Bible is both fascinating and indispensable; for this history and geography are the arena in which God chose to speak and to act.

Medieval Christian geographers believed Jerusalem was at the center of the earth, and their maps illustrated this. In the Church of the Holy Sepulcher, Jerusalem, which was built over the traditional site of Jesus' burial and Resurrection, a stone in the floor marks what was believed to be the world's exact center. Geographically, of course, this is nonsense. Theologically, however, for Christians this is "the Holy Land," a place distinct. It is also the center of world history and geography in the sense that it is the land promised by God to Abraham some two thousand years before the time of Christ. Jesus lived and died here; and the Christian church was formed here, outlasting the Roman Empire and changing the course of world history.

It seems no accident that this land was chosen as the site of salvation history. It forms a kind of bridge between three continents: Africa, Europe, and Asia meet at the eastern end of the Mediterranean and their peoples have always encountered each other on its trade routes. During ancient times, this land was invaded and conquered by armies from all three continents—Egyptian, Assyrian, Babylonian, Persian, Greek, and Roman. God set Jerusalem "in the center of the nations" (Ezekiel 5:5).

THE PROMISED LAND

The wider scene of the arena of Old Testament history is often called the "Fertile Crescent," as it sweeps in a semicircle from Egypt to Mesopotamia, from the Nile valley to the alluvial plain of the Euphrates and Tigris Rivers, enclosing the Arabian desert. This wider region features prominently in the early history of the Jews: God called Abraham from Ur of the Chaldees, situated just nine miles from the River Euphrates in southern Iraq, and Moses from Egypt, where as a baby he narrowly escaped drowning in the River Nile.

When God told Moses that He was to bring His people out of Egypt into Canaan, He described it as "a rich and spacious land, a land flowing with milk and honey" (Exodus 3:8). Similarly, when Moses sent spies to explore the land, they confirmed this description: "The land we passed through and explored is excellent . . . a land flowing with milk and honey" (Numbers 14:7–8). They showed concrete evidence of

The domed roof of the Church of the Holy Sepulcher, Jerusalem.

Part of the Jordan Valley south of Galilee. The Promised Land was often described in the Old Testament as a land "flowing with milk and honey."

their claims, bringing back with them a bunch of grapes so heavy that it had to be slung on a pole carried by two men (Numbers 13:23–24).

Snow-capped Mount Hermon is on the northern border of the Holy Land.

Just before entering the Promised Land, after a delay of forty years brought about by Israel's disobedience, Moses told the people:

" . . . *the Lord your God is bringing you to a rich land—a land with streams and springs, with waters that flow in the valleys and hills; a land with wheat and barley, vines and figs, pomegranates, olives, oil, and honey; a land in which bread will not be scarce and you will want nothing; a land in which the rocks are iron and you can dig copper from the hills*" (Deuteronomy 8:7–9).

Although farmers in this region have to work hard, this is still today a fitting description of the country. The Holy Land extends only about 200 miles from north to south and 100 miles west to east, and is hemmed in by natural boundaries. To the north rise the mountains of Lebanon and Anti-Lebanon; to the west lies the Mediterranean, known in ancient times as "the Great Sea"; and to the east and south lie the barren deserts of Arabia and Zin (Numbers 34:1–15).

In the Bible, the most common expression for the whole country is "from Dan to Beersheba" (Judges 20:1; 1 Samuel 3:20; 2 Samuel 3:10; 1 Kings 4:25)—Dan being Israel's most northerly city, and Beersheba its most southerly, situated at the edge of the desert of Zin (Negeb), about halfway between the Mediterranean and the southern tip of the Dead Sea.

THE FERTILE CRESCENT

As we have seen, the Fertile Crescent is the arc of land running from the Gulf to the Nile Delta, hedged by mountains on the east and north and enclosing the deserts of central Syria and Arabia. Rainfall in those mountains and in the Amanus and the Lebanon ranges along the Mediterranean coast fills the great Tigris and Euphrates Rivers and the lesser Orontes and Jordan. The first two make farming possible in Babylonia and so enabled cities first to arise there six thousand years ago. Rainfall in Ethiopia fills the Nile, giving life to Egypt.

Agriculture in the Fertile Crescent
The earliest farming consisted of grain production in the river regions, while grapes and olives were grown as well in the hilly regions such as the Holy Land. Animals grazed in the fields and on the hillsides, sheep being especially important in Babylonia, where their wool supplied a major textile trade (Joshua 7:21). Horses were raised in the hills of Ararat (eastern Turkey) and Iran, though the usual animal for load-carrying was the donkey. From about 1200 B.C. camel breeding began to be important in Arabia.

The well-irrigated banks of the River Nile form the western end of the Fertile Crescent.

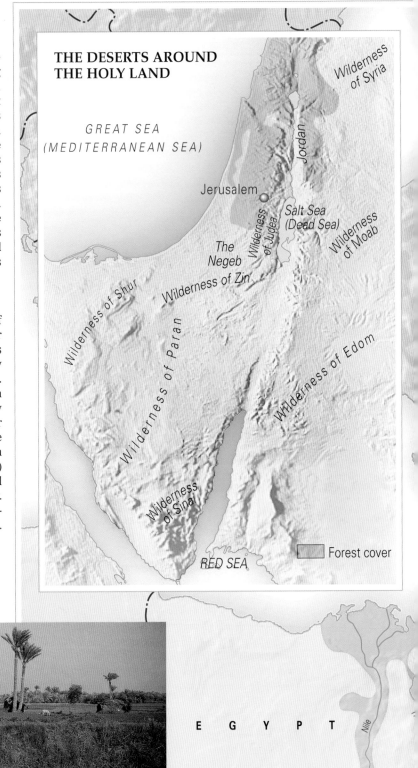

THE DESERTS AROUND THE HOLY LAND

GREAT SEA (MEDITERRANEAN SEA)

Wilderness of Syria

Jerusalem

Salt Sea (Dead Sea)

Jordan

Wilderness of Judea

Wilderness of Moab

The Negeb

Wilderness of Zin

Wilderness of Shur

Wilderness of Paran

Wilderness of Edom

Wilderness of Sinai

RED SEA

Forest cover

E G Y P T

Nile

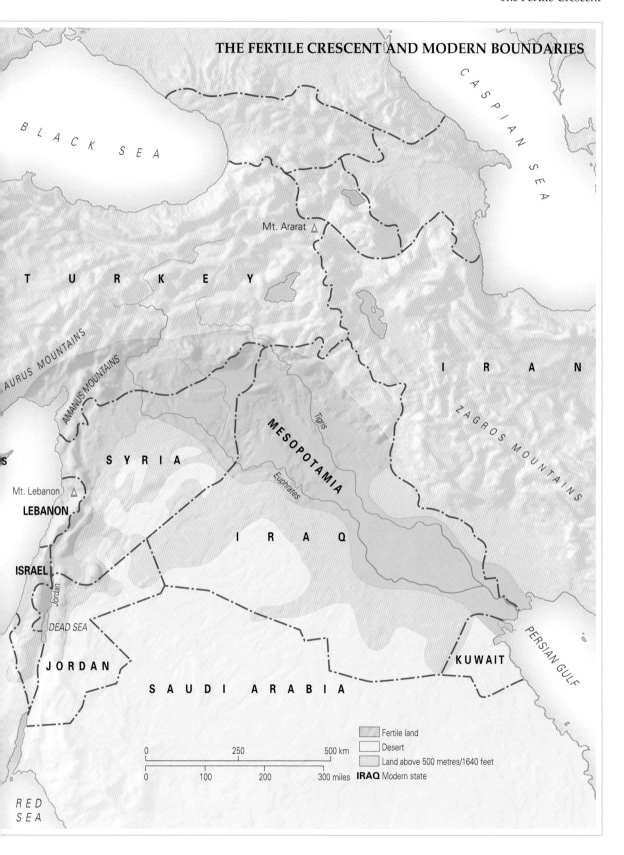

THE FERTILE CRESCENT AND MODERN BOUNDARIES

CASPIAN SEA

BLACK SEA

Mt. Ararat △

TURKEY

TAURUS MOUNTAINS

AMANUS MOUNTAINS

IRAN

ZAGROS MOUNTAINS

Tigris

MESOPOTAMIA

SYRIA

Euphrates

S

Mt. Lebanon △

LEBANON

IRAQ

ISRAEL

Jordan

DEAD SEA

KUWAIT

PERSIAN GULF

JORDAN

SAUDI ARABIA

Fertile land
Desert
Land above 500 metres/1640 feet
IRAQ Modern state

0	250	500 km
0	100	200	300 miles

RED
SEA

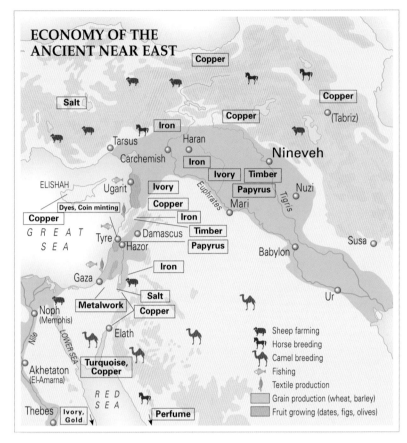

ECONOMY OF THE ANCIENT NEAR EAST

Copper

Salt

Copper

Copper

Iron

(Tabriz)

Tarsus

Haran

Carchemish

Nineveh

Iron

ELISHAH

Ivory

Timber

Ugarit

Ivory

Papyrus

Nuzi

Dyes, Coin minting

Copper

Mari

Copper

Iron

Euphrates

G R E A T

Tyre

Damascus

Timber

S E A

Hazor

Papyrus

Babylon

Tigris

Susa

Iron

Gaza

Ur

Salt

Metalwork

Copper

Noph
(Memphis)

Elath

LOWER SEA

Nile

Turquoise,
Copper

Sheep farming

Horse breeding

Camel breeding

Akhetaton
(El-Amarna)

Fishing

Textile production

R E D
S E A

Grain production (wheat, barley)

Thebes

Ivory,
Gold

Perfume

Fruit growing (dates, figs, olives)

Part of the Holy Land's seacoast, near Ashkelon.

GEOGRAPHY OF THE HOLY LAND

When viewing the Holy Land from the air, the eyes immediately slide down the long, straight corridor of the Jordan Valley, running north-south the entire length, from Mount Hermon to the Arabah. Although it meanders wildly along its lower course, the River Jordan is constrained by high-sided valley walls that form part of the Great Rift Valley. This rift is part of a 4,000-mile geological fault that begins in Syria and ends in Mozambique.

Millions of years ago the subterranean plates, upon which the continents of Africa and Asia rest, shifted toward each other and caused the earth's crust to buckle and fracture. This produced the distinctive features of the Holy Land. Pressure between the two plates caused the sub-surface sediments to bulge and rise in the west, resulting in the Judean hills. In Transjordan, the plate tilted upward to produce the high eastern plateau. Between them the sediment dropped, with the result that the surface of the Dead Sea is some 1,300 feet below sea level, the lowest place on earth.

Natural Resources of the Fertile Crescent

Copper was the major metal from about 5000 B.C. until 1000 B.C. Ores were found in the Arabah and smelted there. Copper was alloyed with tin to make bronze from about 2500 B.C. onward. Iron working developed late in the second millennium and this metal gradually replaced bronze for tools and weapons. Gold was brought from the "Land of Punt" (probably Somalia) to Egypt, and was also found in the south of Egypt itself. Gold was also panned from rivers in western Turkey.

The Dead Sea was a major provider of salt, essential for preserving fish. Along the Mediterranean coast, as well as fishing, there was an important industry in dyeing cloth, notably with the Tyrian purple. Spices and incense came from southern Arabia, the Yemen, although balsam grew in the Jordan Valley. Ivory from African and Syrian elephants was beautifully carved to make veneers and inlays for wooden furniture, a luxurious fashion harshly condemned by the prophet Amos (3:15; 6:4).

Climate and Vegetation

The consequence of this cataclysm for climate and vegetation in the region was huge. Although the Holy Land is only some 45 miles wide, altitudes range from over 3,300 feet in the Judean mountains to minus 1,300 feet at the Dead Sea. The Holy Land boasts a great variety of terrain; for instance, the lakes at the north and south ends of the River Jordan contrast markedly, the color and beauty of Galilee comparing starkly with the heat and desolation around the Dead Sea.

Where the land is low lying, away from the coast, temperatures soar and desert conditions prevail. In the mountains temperatures are cooler and rainfall can support pasture-land or cultivation. Since most of the land north of the Dead Sea is hilly, westerly winds coming off the Mediterranean Sea brought rain, which in Bible times supported large areas of forest. South of the Dead Sea hot dry winds from Africa and Arabia produced deserts.

The Bible itself often refers to various regions into which the Holy Land may be divided. For example, its people are described as living "in the Arabah, in the mountains, in the hill country, in the Negeb and on the coast" (Deuteronomy 1:7). The Arabah is the deep gorge of the Jordan Valley running south to the Gulf of Aqaba. The "mountains" here mean the mountains of Judea, while the "hill country" is the Shephelah district. The Negeb, meaning literally "the dry," is the great southern desert, also known as the wilderness of Zin; and the "coast" is of course along the Mediterranean.

The steep cliffs at the Dead Sea form part of the Great Rift Valley.

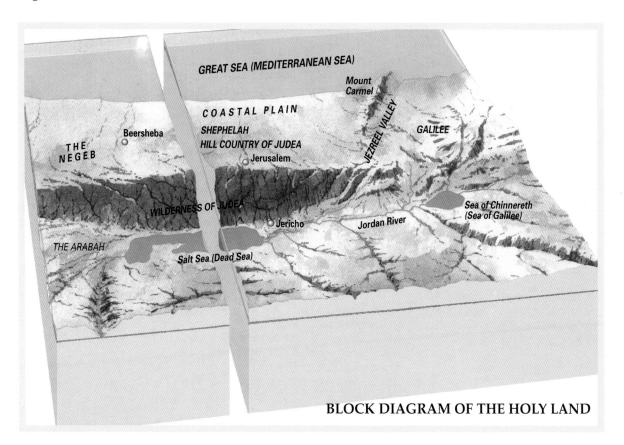

BLOCK DIAGRAM OF THE HOLY LAND

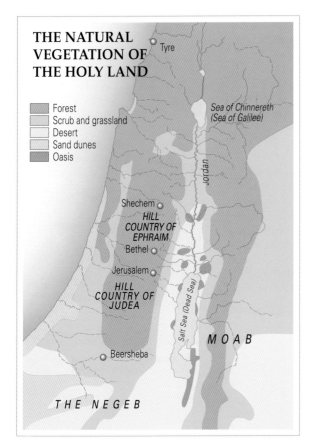

THE NATURAL
VEGETATION OF
THE HOLY LAND

Tyre

Sea of Chinnereth
(Sea of Galilee)

Forest
Scrub and grassland
Desert
Sand dunes
Oasis

Jordan

Shechem

HILL
COUNTRY OF
EPHRAIM

Bethel

Jerusalem

HILL
COUNTRY OF
JUDEA

Salt Sea (Dead Sea)

MOAB

Beersheba

THE NEGEB

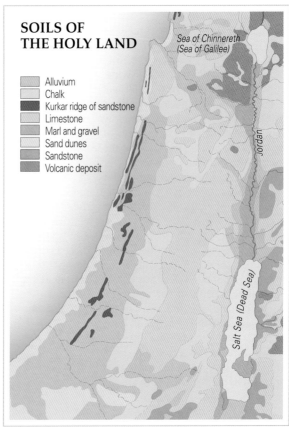

SOILS OF
THE HOLY LAND

Sea of Chinnereth
(Sea of Galilee)

Alluvium
Chalk
Kurkar ridge of sandstone
Limestone
Marl and gravel
Sand dunes
Sandstone
Volcanic deposit

Jordan

Salt Sea (Dead Sea)

THE REGIONS OF THE HOLY LAND

The simplest way to remember the map of the Holy Land is to think of four parallel strips of country running from north to south. As we have seen, the most striking of these is the Jordan Valley. The River Jordan cuts deep between two mountain ranges—the central highlands that form the backbone of the Holy Land (sloping in the west to the coastal plain) and the eastern plateau, beyond which lies the desert. Thus the four strips between the sea and the desert consist of the coastland, the central highlands, the Jordan Valley, and the eastern plateau.

The Coastal Strip

The coastal strip varies in width from a few hundred yards where Mount Carmel juts out into the sea and the port of Haifa is today situated to some 30 miles at the southern end. In ancient times this southern section of the coastal strip was the land of the Philistines, where the five main Philistine cities were located: Gaza, the most southerly, on the ancient road that runs north from Egypt, about three miles inland from the coast; Ashkelon on the coast, twelve miles north; Ashdod, eight miles farther north and on the road again; Ekron, farther north and inland; and Gath in the middle of the plain.

The Shephelah, or foothills, lies immediately east of this Plain of Philistia. In Bible times its sycamore trees were proverbial; Solomon was said to have made "cedars plentiful as sycamores in the foothills" (1 Kings 10:27). The slopes of the Shephelah form the foothills of the central plateau, rising from about 500 feet at Gath to 1,300 feet, 10 miles to the east. At that point the mountains begin, while ten miles east lies Hebron, the highest city in the Holy Land, at 3,300 feet.

Immediately north of the Plain of Philistia, still on the coastal strip, is the Plain of Sharon, of which the main town and port was Joppa (modern Jaffa). In Bible times, this area supported flocks of sheep; we read of the pasturelands of Sharon (1 Chronicles 5:16). However, before modern drainage it must have been very marshy.

RELIEF MAP OF THE HOLY LAND

Tyre

△ Mt. Hermon
(9,232ft / 2,184m)

PLAIN OF PHOENICIA

Dan

UPPER GALILEE

Lake Huleh

SYRIAN DESERT

Hazor

A R A M

Acco

LOWER GALILEE

SEA OF CHINNERETH
(SEA OF GALILEE)

Mt. Carmel
(1,732ft / 528m) △

Tiberias

BASHAN

VALLEY OF JEZREEL

Nazareth

Mt. Tabor
(1,929ft / 588m) △

Yarmuk

△ Mt. Moreh

PLAIN OF ESDRAELON

Megiddo

PLAIN OF SHARON

Mt. Gilboa
(1,630ft / 497m) △

Pella

G I L E A D

GREAT SEA

(MEDITERRANEAN SEA)

Mt. Ebal
(3,083ft / 940m)

Jordan

Samaria

Shechem
△ Mt. Gerizim
(2,889ft / 881m)

Jabb

HILLS OF EPHRAIM

I S R A E L

A M M O N

Joppa

THE ARABAH

Lod

Bethel

Gibeon

Jericho

Gezer

Mt. of Olives
(2,723ft / 830m) △

Heshbon

Jerusalem

Qumran

Mt. Nebo
(2,630ft / 802m) △

Ashkelon

PLAIN OF PHILISTIA

Bethlehem

SHEPHELAH

JUDAH

HILLS OF JUDEA

SALT SEA (DEAD SEA)

Dibon

Gaza

Lachish

Hebron

Arnon

THE JUDEAN WILDERNESS

M O A B

Beersheba

T H E   N E G E B

Zered

THE ARABAH

E D O M

meters	feet
1,000	3,281
500	1,640
200	656
0	0
below sea level	below sea level

0   25   50 km

0   10   20   30 miles

The Central Highlands

The central mountain range of the Holy Land begins in Galilee, whose hills and valleys were the backdrop of Jesus' boyhood and much of His ministry. The peaks of Upper Galilee rise to just over 3,000 feet and from the hills above Nazareth, in Lower Galilee, although only about 1,500 feet high, the Mediterranean Sea is visible on a clear day, just 17 miles to the northwest.

South of Nazareth the ground slopes down gently to a wide alluvial plain, which runs southeast from the Mediterranean north of Mount Carmel to the River Jordan. The western part of this area is known as the Plain of Esdraelon; the eastern part as the Valley of Jezreel, lying between the once actively volcanic Mount Moreh and the limestone Mount Gilboa. On the slopes of these mountains the opposing armies of Philistines and Israelites encamped, facing each other across the valley, before the battle in which King Saul died (1 Samuel 31:1; 2 Samuel 1:17, 19, 21).

The stronghold of Megiddo stands in the middle of the southern edge of

Part of the Judean Wilderness, where Jesus was tempted by the devil.

the Plain of Esdraelon, at the foot of the Carmel range. For centuries it has guarded the entrance to the main pass through the mountains to the south. Megiddo was one of the cities that King Solomon rebuilt and fortified to house his war-horses and chariots (1 Kings 9:15, 19).

South of the Plain of Esdraelon lies the hill country of Manasseh and Ephraim, covered with vineyards on its west-facing slopes; and

farther south again the hill country of Judah. These two mountainous regions were at the center of Israel's history during the time of the divided monarchy; the capital of the Northern Kingdom was Samaria (in Manasseh-Ephraim), and the capital of the Southern Kingdom was Jerusalem (in Judah).

Jerusalem is built on a mountain and surrounded by mountains. "As the mountains surround Jerusalem, so the Lord surrounds His people," the Psalmist wrote (Psalms 48:1–2; 125:2). Immediately east of Jerusalem across the Kidron Valley lies the Mount of Olives, and from its summit the road runs east through barren land, dropping more than 3,000 feet to Jericho and the Dead Sea. While making this journey on foot, the traveler in Jesus' parable was attacked by thieves and rescued by the Good Samaritan. This area between Jerusalem and the Dead Sea is known as the Judean Wilderness; and here Jesus spent forty days being tempted by the devil, following His Baptism.

Part of the Plain of Esdraelon (or Jezreel) from the slopes of Mount Tabor.

The Jordan Valley

As we have seen, the Jordan Valley forms part of the Great Rift Valley, which stretches for 4,000 miles from Asia Minor through the Red Sea to the Rift Valley of East Africa. However, the River Jordan itself is only 80 miles in length, not counting its meanderings. It rises in Mount Hermon, a 9,000-foot shoulder of the Anti-Lebanon mass, and descends steadily ("Jordan" literally means "descender") through Lake Huleh and Lake Tiberias before finally emptying into the Dead Sea. At Huleh it is about 230 feet above sea level, but Lake Tiberias (Galilee) is nearly 700 feet below, and the Dead Sea about 1,300 feet below. The bottom of the Dead Sea is more than 2,500 feet below sea level, and the lowest point on the earth's surface.

In the Bible Lake Huleh is known as "the Waters of Merom" (Joshua 11:5–7), and it has always been rich in birds. Today much of it has been drained for agricultural land, while other parts form a nature reserve.

In the Gospels, Lake Tiberias is sometimes called "the Sea of Kinnereth/Chinnereth" (or Gennesaret), or "the Sea of Galilee." It is only 12 miles long and at its widest 7 miles across; but it is deep and full of fish. Jesus' first disciples, the brothers Andrew and Simon, James and John, sustained a fishing business there. Although the lake is almost completely surrounded by hills, in Bible times numerous fishing towns and villages that Jesus visited during His ministry were located around its north and west shores.

South of the Sea of Galilee the Jordan flows another 65 miles before reaching the Dead Sea. For much of this distance it is unimpressive and muddy, as Naaman, the Syrian general suffering from leprosy, recognized: "Are not the Abana and the Pharpar, the rivers of Damascus, better than any of the waters of Israel?" (2 Kings 5:12). Lions were known to lurk in the thick jungle of this part of the river valley in Bible times (Jeremiah 49:19). The Baptismal site of John the Baptist is unknown, but it was possibly at one of the fords near where the Jordan enters the Dead Sea (Mark 1:5).

In the Old Testament the entire Rift Valley is called "the Arabah," meaning "dry," and the Dead Sea is called the "Sea of the Arabah" or "Salt Sea." It is 48 miles long and incredibly desolate. Its eastern shore is overlooked by the steep mountains of Moab, while the barren slopes of the mountains of Judah lie to the west. Here, at Qumran around the time of Christ, lived the Essene monastic community, and here in 1947 the Dead Sea Scrolls were found in some of the caves in the nearby hills.

The heat here is so intense, up to 110° F in summer, the evaporation so great and the rainfall so small, that the water-level of the Dead Sea remains constant despite the inflowing water and the absence of any outflow. As a result, the chemical deposits such as sodium, potassium, and magnesium in the water are highly concentrated, and no fish can survive (Ezekiel 47:1–12). Sodom and Gomorrah, "the cities of the plain," were thought to have been located in the area now covered by the southern tip of the Dead Sea, and perhaps the brimstone and fire that rained on them resulted from an earthquake and volcanic eruption (Genesis 19:24–29).

The Arabah continues south of the Dead Sea until it reaches the Red Sea at the Gulf of Aqaba. Here in Bible times stood the port of Ezion-geber (modern Eilat), which allowed Israel maritime access to trade with Africa and Asia (1 Kings 9:26). Copper was exported from the nearby mines at Timna, which Solomon developed, and imports included such exotic items as gold, silver, and ivory, and apes and baboons (1 Kings 10:22).

Hills surround the Sea of Galilee, viewed here from the north, near Capernaum.

The Eastern Plateau

The fourth strip of the Holy Land is the eastern plateau, between the Jordan Valley and the Arabian Desert. This area was inherited by two and a half of Israel's twelve tribes: Gad, Reuben, and the half-tribe of Manasseh (Joshua 18:7).

This is a vast plateau, stretching for about 250 miles from north to south, and divided by four rivers, which have cut deep canyons on their way west to the River Jordan or Dead Sea: the River Yarmuk, flowing into the Jordan just south of Lake Tiberias; the River Jabbok, reaching the Jordan about halfway between Lake Chinnereth (the Sea of Galilee) and the Dead Sea; the River Arnon, flowing into the middle of the Dead Sea; and the River Zered, emptying into its southern tip. These rivers formed natural borders for Israel's neighbors: Ammon claimed the territory between the Jabbok and the Arnon; Moab that between the Arnon and the Zered—though often spilling over to the north; and Edom the territory south of the Zered.

South of Bashan was Gilead, the name for almost the whole of Transjordan between Lake Tiberias and the Dead Sea. As the land rises to above 3,000 feet, rainfall is considerable, making for fertile forests and vineyards. The grapes of Gilead were the best in the Holy Land and balm of Gilead—an aromatic spice—was famous. The camel-train of Ishmaelites to whom his brothers sold Joseph was loaded with spices, balm, and myrrh from Gilead (Genesis 37:25).

Continuing on south through Transjordan, next comes Ammon and then Moab, occupying the mountainous region east of the Dead Sea. Apart from the deep gorges of the River Arnon and of some smaller streams, most of Moab is a high plateau, sometimes called "the land of the shepherd." It was from Mount Nebo, in the mountains of Moab, that Moses looked into the Promised

RIVERS AND STREAMS OF THE HOLY LAND

Land before he died; and on the plains of Moab that the children of Israel encamped before crossing the Jordan to take possession of that land (Deuteronomy 32:49–50; 34:1–8; Numbers 22:1).

Edom is the most southerly section of Transjordan. Rising to about 3,500 feet at its highest points, it towers over the deserts to the west, east, and south. Through Edom passed the great eastern trade route known as "the King's Highway" (see p. 17). Because Edom refused to al- low the Israelites to use this route on their way to the Promised Land, long-standing enmity arose between the two peoples (Numbers 20:14–21; 21:4).

THE AGRICULTURE OF THE HOLY LAND

The traditional economy of the Holy Land was agricultural. Pastoralism predominated on the higher and poorer ground, while arable farming was practiced in the valleys, where at least 8 inches of rain would fall annually. Rivalry for land was frequently a source of conflict in the Old Testament, as illustrated in the stories of Abraham and Lot.

Israelite livestock consisted mostly of sheep and goats, which roamed in mixed flocks over the hills. The goats supplied milk and the black hair from which tents were constructed, while the sheep gave milk, meat, and wool. Because shepherds kept their sheep more for wool than for meat, a close relationship often grew between sheep and shepherd. The shepherd would lead his sheep, rather than drive them, so that the Psalmist could say: "The Lord is my shepherd, I shall not be in want. He makes me lie down in verdant pastures, he leads me to quiet waters" (Psalm 23:1–2).

However, even more Israelite farmers cultivated the soil. The three main products of the Holy Land—grain, wine, and oil—are often grouped together in the Bible (Deuteronomy 7:13; Psalm 104:15; Joel 2:19). The grains from which their bread came were mostly wheat and barley; the wine came from the extensive vineyards; and the oil—mainly for cooking—from the olive groves. Olive trees are particularly hardy, able to survive in shallow soil and withstand long periods of drought.

Other fruits of ancient Israel include pomegranates, and especially figs (Micah 4:4). A poor fruit could be obtained by slitting the husks of the sycamore tree (Amos 7:14). For a good harvest, the land was very dependent upon rain (Acts 14:15–17; Matthew 5:45).

THE CLIMATE OF THE HOLY LAND

Warm air from the Mediterranean brings mild winters to the coastal zone, and it is in this season that more than 90 percent of the rainfall comes; but in the hills and mountains the temperature can drop below freezing, and snow may fall in places such as Jerusalem. Summers—from May to September—are hot and dry, with temperatures soaring to over 100° F in the Jordan Valley and beside the Dead Sea. During the dry season there are only dew and morning mist to bring moisture, but both disappear rapidly when the sun rises (Hosea 13:3).

A transitional steppe climate bridges the area between the mild Mediterranean zone and the harsh, arid conditions of the desert. In this zone, roughly between Hebron and Beersheba and on the western edge of the Transjordan plateau, 8–10 inches of rain will fall in a year, while the desert areas beyond will generally have under 8 inches per year.

A bedouin shepherd with his mixed flock of sheep and goats in the barren hills of Judea, east of Bethlehem.

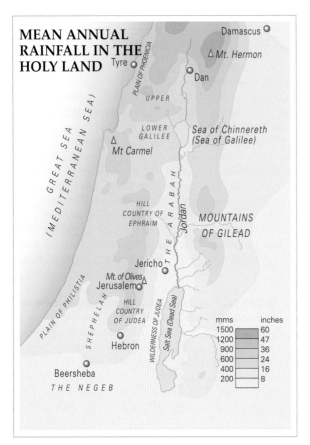

MEAN ANNUAL RAINFALL IN THE HOLY LAND

mms	inches
1500	60
1200	47
900	36
600	24
400	16
200	8

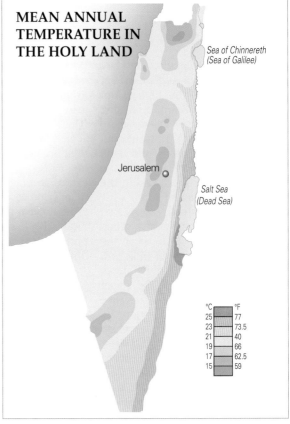

MEAN ANNUAL TEMPERATURE IN THE HOLY LAND

°C	°F
25	77
23	73.5
21	40
19	66
17	62.5
15	59

The Rains

The beginning of the rainy season was usually called "the early rains," which were looked upon as indispensable. Without them, plowing was impossible, for the sun-baked earth was too hard (Deuteronomy 28:23). But once the rains had begun to soften the soil—especially if they came late—the farmer of Bible times had to brave the storms and get on with plowing.

While the early rains at the start of the rainy season (November onward) were essential for plowing, the "later rains" at its end (March–April) were essential for a good harvest. Without them, the corn remained thin and desiccated.

So the early and late rain, sometimes called the autumn rain and the spring rain, were both necessary for a good harvest. Wise farmers knew this and waited for the valuable crop of the earth, remaining patient until it received "the autumn and spring rains" (James 5:7).

THREE ANNUAL FESTIVALS

In view of Israel's closeness to the soil, it is not surprising that their three annual festivals had both agricultural and religious significance.

About the middle of April the Feast of the Passover, followed by the Feast of Unleavened Bread, commemorated Israel's liberation from Egypt, but also included the waving of the first sheaf of ripe barley.

The second great festival was the Feast of the Firstfruits, or Harvest, also known as the Feast of Weeks, or Pentecost. This was the feast of thanksgiving for the grain harvest that had been safely gathered in. It also came to commemorate the giving of the Law at Mount Sinai.

The last of the three annual festivals was the Feast of Booths, or Tabernacles. For seven days the people had to live in shelters made from branches so that they knew that "the people of Israel lived in booths when I brought them out of Egypt" (Leviticus 23:39–43). This festival was also known as the Ingathering, for it took place in mid-October, six months after Passover, by which time the produce of the vineyards and olive groves as well as the fields had been gathered.

The three feasts were all originally harvest festivals to which historic events were tied. They marked, respectively, the beginning of the barley harvest, the end of the grain harvest, and the end of the fruit harvest.

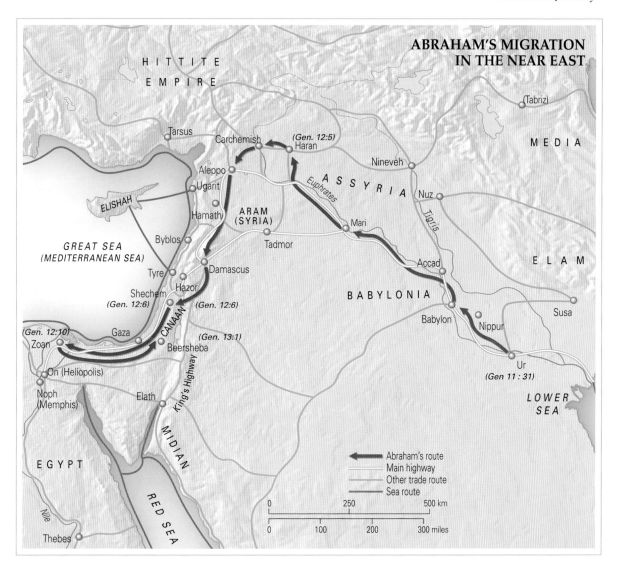

ABRAHAM'S MIGRATION IN THE NEAR EAST

Abraham's route
Main highway
Other trade route
Sea route

0   250   500 km

0   100   200   300 miles

The Old Testament

Christians divide history into B.C. and A.D., indicating the periods before and after Christ, Jesus Christ's coming into the world forming the watershed of history. Similarly, the life of Jesus divides the Bible in half, the Old Testament looking forward to His arrival and preparing for it, the New Testament telling the story of His life, death, and Resurrection, and spelling out their implications in the infant Church.

ABRAHAM'S JOURNEYS

Abraham's journeys began when his father Terah took him from Ur of the Chaldees in southern Iraq, a major trading city and center for the worship of the moon-god Sin. Abraham's family then settled in Haran, another worship center and city devoted to Sin. (Abraham later sent Eliezer to this area to find Isaac a wife, showing the importance of family ties for the patriarchs.) Some time after 2000 B.C. God called Abraham to leave his country and people for another country and another people that God would give him (Genesis 12:1–3).

God promised Abraham a land and many descendants. And He promised, "I will be their God" (Genesis 17:3–8). The rest of the Old Testament and the whole of the New Testament are a working out of these promises of God. God kept renewing His covenant with Abraham during his lifetime, and then confirmed it to his son Isaac and to his grandson Jacob. In Old Testament days Israel was the promised seed and Canaan the Promised Land.

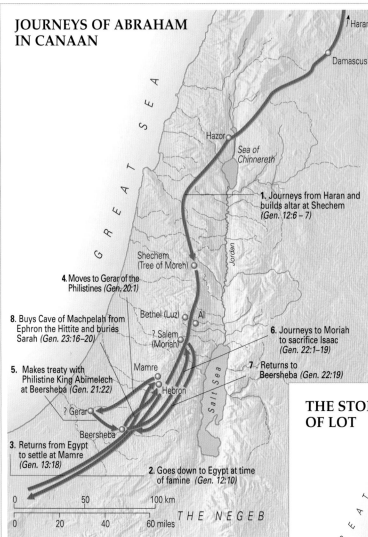

JOURNEYS OF ABRAHAM IN CANAAN

GREAT SEA

Haran

Damascus

Hazor

Sea of Chinnereth

Jordan

1. Journeys from Haran and builds altar at Shechem *(Gen. 12:6 – 7)*

Shechem (Tree of Moreh)

4. Moves to Gerar of the Philistines *(Gen. 20:1)*

Bethel (Luz) Ai

8. Buys Cave of Machpelah from Ephron the Hittite and buries Sarah *(Gen. 23:16–20)*

? Salem (Moriah)

6. Journeys to Moriah to sacrifice Isaac *(Gen. 22:1–19)*

Mamre

7. Returns to Beersheba *(Gen. 22:19)*

5. Makes treaty with Philistine King Abimelech at Beersheba *(Gen. 21:22)*

Hebron

Salt Sea

? Gerar

Beersheba

3. Returns from Egypt to settle at Mamre *(Gen. 13:18)*

2. Goes down to Egypt at time of famine *(Gen. 12:10)*

0   50   100 km
0   20   40   60 miles

THE NEGEB

gave Abraham at Salem, and God's intervention as he was about to sacrifice Isaac on Mount Moriah, point to the later importance of Jerusalem in Jewish history, for Salem is believed to be Jerusalem and Mount Moriah the hill on which the Temple stood.

THE PATRIARCHS

The land promised to the patriarchs was in the Bronze Age, but they never settled down to enjoy it, as they were nomads. Abraham and Isaac stayed in southern Canaan, in the area of Hebron, where the burial cave was, and near the Philistines of Gerar. Esau settled in southern Transjordan, in the Mount Seir region of Edom. The patriarchs Abraham, Isaac, and Jacob all maintained links with Haran far to the north.

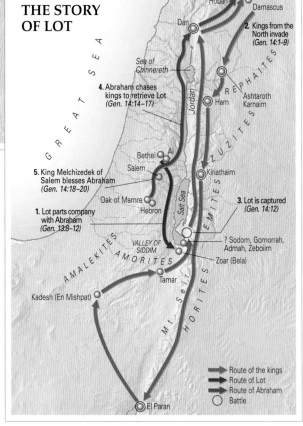

THE STORY OF LOT

GREAT SEA

Hobah

Damascus

Dan

2. Kings from the North invade *(Gen. 14:1–9)*

Sea of Chinnereth

REPHAITES

Ham

Ashtaroth Karnaim

Jordan

4. Abraham chases kings to retrieve Lot *(Gen. 14:14–17)*

ZUZITES

Bethel Ai

Salem

Kiriathaim

5. King Melchizedek of Salem blesses Abraham *(Gen. 14:18–20)*

Oak of Mamre

Hebron

Salt Sea

EMITES

3. Lot is captured *(Gen. 14:12)*

1. Lot parts company with Abraham *(Gen. 13:8–12)*

VALLEY OF SIDDIM

? Sodom, Gomorrah, Admah, Zeboiim

AMALEKITES

AMORITES

Zoar (Bela)

Tamar

HORITES

Mt Seir

Kadesh (En Mishpat)

Route of the kings
Route of Lot
Route of Abraham
○ Battle

El Paran

Although Abraham now spent many years in Canaan and never returned to Mesopotamia, he made one further journey, following the road to Egypt, which the caravans traveled bearing goods from Syria.

By 2000 B.C. there were in the Promised Land, Canaan, both city-dwellers and pastoralists who migrated in search of new pastures. Abraham never settled in a city, but by purchasing the Cave of Machpelah as a burial place he laid claim to the land. Various tribes lived there, called generally Canaanites, among them the Hittites who sold Abraham the cave. They may have been linked to the powerful Hittites who ruled Anatolia (northern Turkey) from about 1800 to 1200 B.C. Abraham's career made another place in Canaan important to his descendants. The blessing King Melchizedek

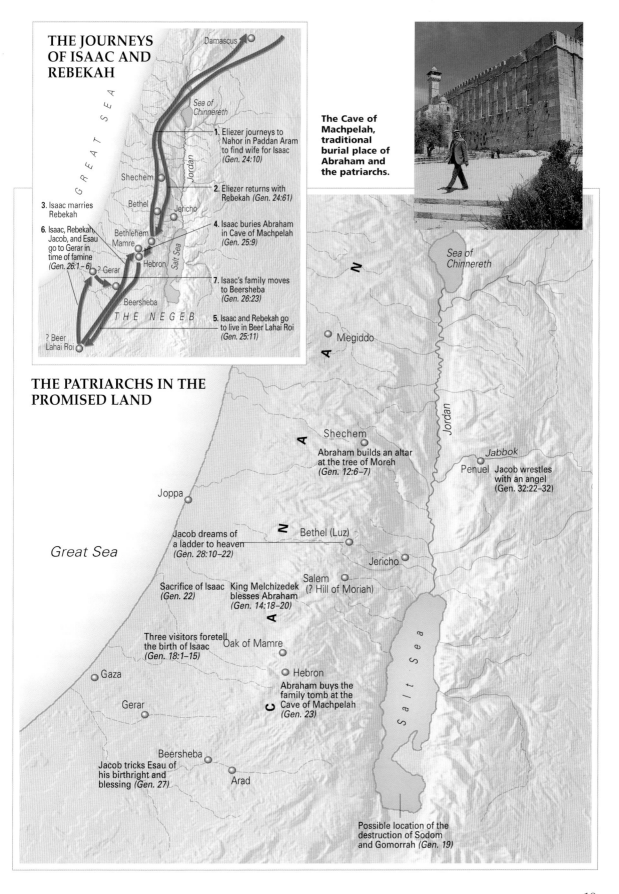

THE JOURNEYS OF ISAAC AND REBEKAH

1. Eliezer journeys to Nahor in Paddan Aram to find wife for Isaac (Gen. 24:10)

2. Eliezer returns with Rebekah (Gen. 24:61)

3. Isaac marries Rebekah

4. Isaac buries Abraham in Cave of Machpelah (Gen. 25:9)

6. Isaac, Rebekah, Jacob, and Esau go to Gerar in time of famine (Gen. 26:1–6)

7. Isaac's family moves to Beersheba (Gen. 26:23)

5. Isaac and Rebekah go to live in Beer Lahai Roi (Gen. 25:11)

Damascus

Sea of Chinnereth

GREAT SEA

Jordan

Shechem

Bethel

Jericho

Bethlehem

Mamre

Hebron

Salt Sea

? Gerar

Beersheba

THE NEGEB

? Beer Lahai Roi

The Cave of Machpelah, traditional burial place of Abraham and the patriarchs.

THE PATRIARCHS IN THE PROMISED LAND

Great Sea

Megiddo

Sea of Chinnereth

Jordan

Jabbok

Penuel Jacob wrestles with an angel (Gen. 32:22–32)

Shechem
Abraham builds an altar at the tree of Moreh (Gen. 12:6–7)

Joppa

Bethel (Luz)
Jacob dreams of a ladder to heaven (Gen. 28:10–22)

Jericho

Salem
(? Hill of Moriah)

Sacrifice of Isaac (Gen. 22)

King Melchizedek blesses Abraham (Gen. 14:18–20)

Three visitors foretell the birth of Isaac (Gen. 18:1–15)

Oak of Mamre

Gaza

Hebron
Abraham buys the family tomb at the Cave of Machpelah (Gen. 23)

Gerar

Beersheba
Jacob tricks Esau of his birthright and blessing (Gen. 27)

Arad

Salt Sea

Possible location of the destruction of Sodom and Gomorrah (Gen. 19)

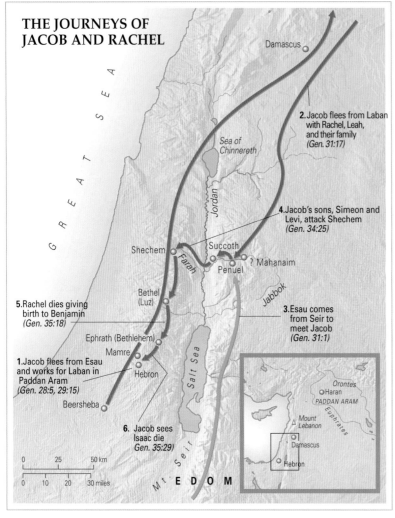

THE JOURNEYS OF JACOB AND RACHEL

Damascus

2. Jacob flees from Laban with Rachel, Leah, and their family (Gen. 31:17)

Sea of Chinnereth

Jordan

4. Jacob's sons, Simeon and Levi, attack Shechem (Gen. 34:25)

G R E A T   S E A

Shechem
Farah
Succoth
Penuel
? Mahanaim

Bethel (Luz)
Jabbok

5. Rachel dies giving birth to Benjamin (Gen. 35:18)

3. Esau comes from Seir to meet Jacob (Gen. 31:1)

Ephrath (Bethlehem)
Mamre

Salt Sea

1. Jacob flees from Esau and works for Laban in Paddan Aram (Gen. 28:5, 29:15)

Hebron

Beersheba

6. Jacob sees Isaac die Gen. 35:29)

0   25   50 km
0   10   20   30 miles

Orontes
Haran
PADDAN ARAM

Euphrates

Mount Lebanon

Damascus

Hebron

Seir

Mt E D O M

ISRAEL IN EGYPT

Jacob (whose other name was "Israel") had twelve sons, who were the original "children of Israel." But these progenitors of Israel's twelve tribes all spent their last years and died not in Canaan, but in Egypt, to which they were driven by famine. Joseph became a very senior administrator in Egypt and also died in exile there (Genesis 50:26). The stories of Joseph and his brothers agree with other evidence for Semitic people living in the Nile Delta area, especially between about 2000 and 1550 B.C. The circumstances of that period agree better than any other with the way of life and events the patriarchal narratives describe.

Exodus 1:8 states "a new king, who knew nothing of Joseph, rose to power in Egypt"; one of the succeeding dynasties is meant, probably the nineteenth, whose early pharaohs built the cities Pithom and Rameses, the latter as a royal residence in the Delta area where the Israelites had settled. The pharaohs were worried that the Israelites might collaborate with other Semitic invaders. It became convenient, therefore, to use Israelites as slave labor. As the years passed, the bondage of the Israelites became harder to bear (Exodus 1:14). The Egyptian exile probably lasted altogether 430 years (Exodus 12:40–41).

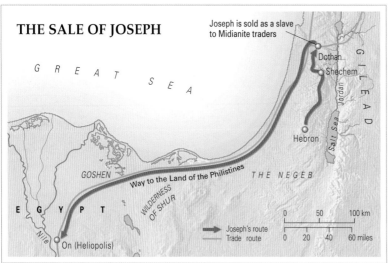

THE SALE OF JOSEPH

Joseph is sold as a slave to Midianite traders

G R E A T   S E A

Dothan
Shechem

G I L E A D

Jordan

GOSHEN
Way to the Land of the Philistines
THE NEGEB

Hebron

Salt Sea

WILDERNESS OF SHUR

E G Y P T

Nile

On (Heliopolis)

Joseph's route
Trade route

0   50   100 km
0   20   40   60 miles

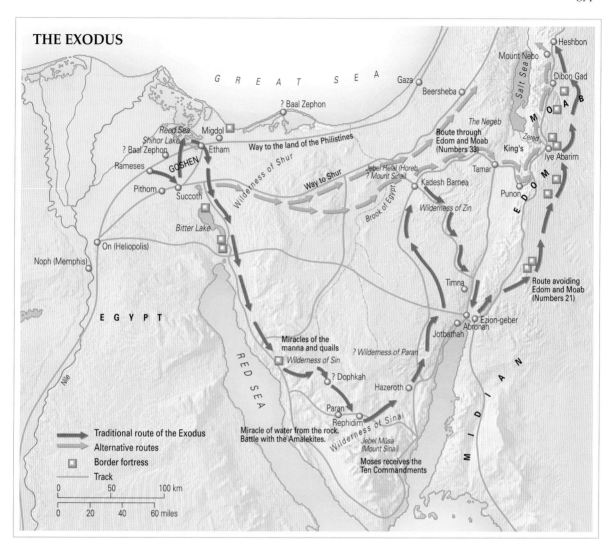

THE EXODUS

Heshbon
Mount Nebo
Salt Sea
Dibon Gad
Gaza
MOAB
Beersheba
? Baal Zephon
The Negeb
Route through Edom and Moab (Numbers 33)
Reed Sea   Migdol
Shihor Lake   Etham   Way to the land of the Philistines
? Baal Zephon   King's
Zered
Rameses   GOSHEN   Wilderness of Shur   Iye Abarim
Jebel Helal (Horeb, ? Mount Sinai)   Tamar
Pithom   Way to Shur   Kadesh Barnea   EDOM
Succoth   Brook of Egypt
Punon
Bitter Lake   Wilderness of Zin
On (Heliopolis)
Noph (Memphis)
Route avoiding Edom and Moab (Numbers 21)
Timna
EGYPT
Ezion-geber
Abronah
Jotbathah
Miracles of the manna and quails
Wilderness of Sin   ? Wilderness of Paran
RED SEA
? Dophkah
Hazeroth
Paran   Wilderness of Sinai
Nile   Rephidim
Miracle of water from the rock.   MIDIAN
Battle with the Amalekites.   Jebel Mûsa (Mount Sinai)
Moses receives the Ten Commandments

Traditional route of the Exodus
Alternative routes
Border fortress
Track

| 0 | 50 | 100 km |
| 0 | 20 | 40 | 60 miles |

THE EXODUS FROM EGYPT

As the people of Israel groaned under the pharaohs' oppressive regime, they cried to God for deliverance (Exodus 2:24). Moses had been brought up in the Egyptian court (Exodus 2:1–10) and learned the wisdom of the Egyptians. But he had to flee for his life and hid in the Sinai peninsula (Exodus 2:11–22). Near Mount Horeb (or Sinai), where he later received the Ten Commandments, God spoke to Moses from the burning bush (Exodus 3:1–6), telling him he was to rescue

the people of Israel and bring them into the Promised Land. Moses was commissioned to go to pharaoh and demand his people's release.

The people of Israel accepted Moses' leadership, but pharaoh, probably Rameses II who reigned over Egypt for sixty-six years (1290–1224 B.C.), demurred. Not until after the ten plagues did he finally consent (Exodus 4:27–13:16), c. 1280 B.C.

The escaping Israelites did not travel direct to the Promised Land along the coastal route known as "The Way to the Land of the Philistines" (Exodus 13:17–18), as it was heavily fortified. The route

taken is debated. The traditional route runs from Rameses to Succoth, and then turns northward to cross the Reed Sea, a marshy lake north of the northern tip of the Suez Gulf (Exodus 14:21). After this, they turned southeast to Mount Sinai.

The locations of some of the places visited by the Israelites during the wilderness period are uncertain. The traditional site of Mount Sinai is Jebel Musa; however, an alternative opinion places it at Jebel Helal in north Sinai. If this were so, the Israelites would have taken the Way to Shur, a much shorter journey to Canaan, via Beersheba.

It took the Israelites about three months to reach Mount Sinai, and they stayed there almost a year. Here God gave Israel three gifts: a renewed covenant, a moral law, and a system of sacrifices. The moral law was the Ten Commandments, supplemented by other statutes and judgments. The new covenant was ratified by sacrifice, when the people gave an undertaking to keep the law.

God also gave instructions for the building of a "tabernacle," a rectangular tent, situated in a large courtyard, measuring about 45 feet by 15 feet, made of dyed linen curtains stretched over a frame and covered with goats' hair and waterproof skins, inside which were two rooms, "the holy place" and "the most holy place," or "holy of holies." Its fabric, furniture, and construction are described in Exodus 25–27, 30, and 35–40; the five main sacrifices are explained in Leviticus 1–7; and full details of the dress and duties of the priests are given in Exodus 28–29 and in Leviticus.

WILDERNESS WANDERINGS

The tabernacle was first erected on the anniversary of the Israelites' escape from Egypt (Exodus 40:17). Two weeks later the Passover was celebrated (Numbers 9:1–3), and a fortnight later again a census taken of all the men fit to serve as soldiers (Numbers 1:1–3). Soon afterward, the march began. The tabernacle was dismantled and the Israelites set out from Sinai (Numbers 10:11–12). At last, some seven centuries after it had first been made to Abraham, God's promise to give His people the land of Canaan seemed about to be fulfilled (Numbers 10:29).

But such expectations were short-lived. First, the people complained about the shortage of food (Numbers 11:1–6), then Miriam and Aaron, Moses' sister and brother, undermined his authority (Numbers 12). Finally, twelve spies whom Moses sent out to reconnoiter Canaan reported it was a land flowing with milk and honey, but added that its inhabitants were invincible (Numbers 13:27–29, 31). Two of the spies, Caleb and Joshua, pleaded with the people not to disbelieve God. But God's judgment on His people meant that no adult of that generation was to enter the land of promise except Caleb and Joshua.

Forty years elapsed between the exodus from Egypt and the entry into Canaan, many of which seem to have been spent at the oasis of Kadesh-barnea in the Negeb. But the children of Israel also wandered down south to Sinai again, then north and east through rugged Edomite territory south of the Dead Sea. From here they could have joined the King's Highway, which ran from the Gulf of Aqaba east of the Dead Sea right up into Syria, but the Edomites would not allow them to cross their territory by this route, so they had to skirt farther east around it (Numbers 20:14–21).

To the north were the Amorites, also blocking the King's Highway, under Sihon King of Heshbon and Og King of Bashan. They were

The Sinai Wilderness, near Mount Sinai, where the Ten Commandments were given to Moses.

defeated in battle, and the attempts of the King of Moab to overthrow Israel thwarted (Numbers 21–25). Israel was now encamped on the plains of Moab, close to the River Jordan, north of where it flows into the Dead Sea. Here Moses addressed the people for the last time; his words are recorded in Deuteronomy. He recalled the years of wandering, and reminded the people of God's covenant (Deuteronomy 7:6; 10:12–13).

For forty years Moses had served God and the people of God as lawgiver, administrator, judge, and spokesman of God. His death is recorded at the end of Deuteronomy. He was buried on Mount Nebo by God Himself (Deuteronomy 34:6).

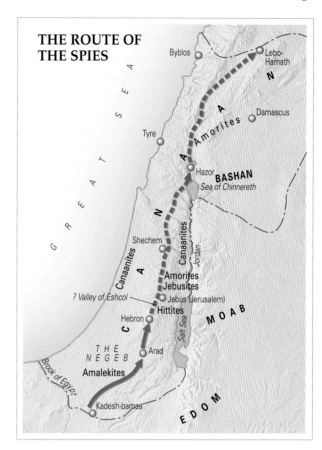

An artist's impression of the tabernacle used by the Israelites during their wilderness wanderings.

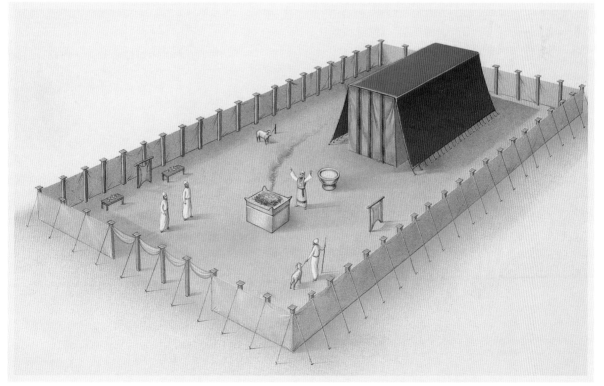

ISRAEL SETTLES IN CANAAN

Already, before his death, Moses had appointed Joshua to lead the people into the Promised Land. Now God's charge came to Joshua: "Be strong and stand firm; you will lead these people to possess the land I promised their fathers to give them" (Joshua 1:6).

Joshua led the Israelites across the River Jordan, opposite Abel-shittim, and set up camp at Gilgal (Joshua 4:19). (One might notice that the version of the conquest in the Book of Joshua is more optimistic than the version found in the Book of Judges. The former account is how the authors of the Bible wished it had gone; Judges is how it actually occurred.)

From here, Joshua conducted his campaigns in the south of Canaan. Before the Israelites stood the ancient walled city of Jericho; its destruction was their first victory in the Promised Land. After initial defeat at Ai, due to Achan's disobedience in stealing loot, the victorious Israelites turned south. Following the capture of Jericho and Ai, the Gibeonites signed a peace treaty with the Israelites. To counter this, the king of Jerusalem formed a coalition with the kings of Hebron, Jarmuth, Lachish, and Eglon, and attacked Gibeon. Joshua's army supported Gibeon in the battle, and pursued the enemy to Makkedah. Many enemy soldiers were killed by huge hailstones, and after the battle the sun stood in the middle of the sky for a full day (Joshua 10:1–15). The Israelites swept on to conquer the southern hill country up to the borders of Philistia.

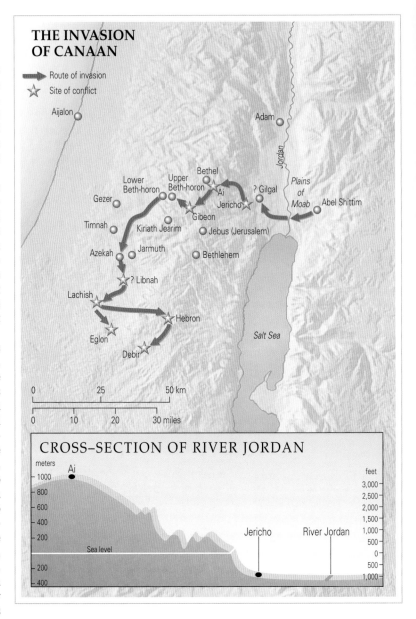

THE INVASION OF CANAAN

➤ Route of invasion
☆ Site of conflict

Aijalon
Adam
Bethel
Lower Beth-horon
Upper Beth-horon
Ai
? Gilgal
Plains of Moab
Abel Shittim
Gezer
Jericho
Jordan
Timnah
Kiriath Jearim
Gibeon
Jebus (Jerusalem)
Azekah
Jarmuth
Bethlehem
? Libnah
Lachish
Hebron
Salt Sea
Eglon
Debir

0   25   50 km
0   10   20   30 miles

CROSS–SECTION OF RIVER JORDAN

meters
1000
800
600
400
200
Sea level
200
400

Ai

feet
3,000
2,500
2,000
1,500
1,000
500
0
500
1,000

Jericho   River Jordan

Next the Israelites turned north, where a coalition commanded by Jabin, King of Hazor, gathered near Lake Huleh for the most important battle in the conquest of northern Canaan (Joshua 11:1–11). Although the enemy army was equipped with horses and chariots—for Israel's settlement in Canaan coincided with the beginning of the Iron Age—it, too, was defeated, and Hazor, the largest city in Canaan in this period, was burned.

THE BATTLE OF AI

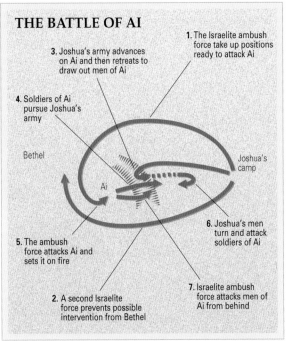

1. The Israelite ambush force take up positions ready to attack Ai

3. Joshua's army advances on Ai and then retreats to draw out men of Ai

4. Soldiers of Ai pursue Joshua's army

Bethel

Joshua's camp

Ai

6. Joshua's men turn and attack soldiers of Ai

5. The ambush force attacks Ai and sets it on fire

7. Israelite ambush force attacks men of Ai from behind

2. A second Israelite force prevents possible intervention from Bethel

THE RESCUE OF GIBEON

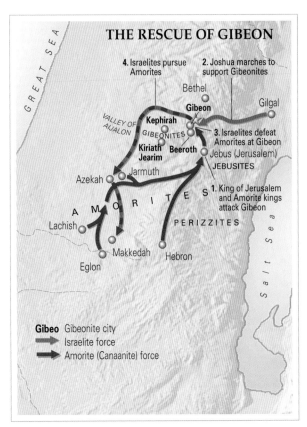

GREAT SEA

4. Israelites pursue Amorites

2. Joshua marches to support Gibeonites

Bethel

Gilgal

Gibeon

Kephirah

VALLEY OF AIJALON

GIBEONITES

3. Israelites defeat Amorites at Gibeon

Kiriath Jearim

Beeroth

Jebus (Jerusalem)

JEBUSITES

Azekah

Jarmuth

1. King of Jerusalem and Amorite kings attack Gibeon

A M O R I T E S

PERIZZITES

Lachish

Salt sea

Makkedah

Hebron

Eglon

Gibeo Gibeonite city

Israelite force

Amorite (Canaanite) force

THE CAPTURE OF HAZOR

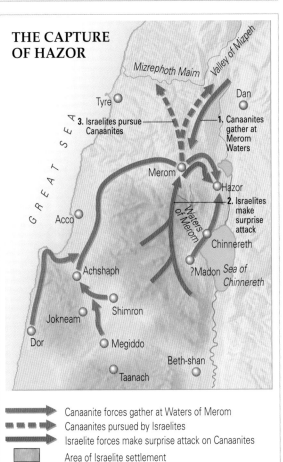

Valley of Mizpeh

Mizrephoth Maim

Tyre

Dan

3. Israelites pursue Canaanites

1. Canaanites gather at Merom Waters

GREAT SEA

Merom

Hazor

2. Israelites make surprise attack

Acco

Waters of Merom

Chinnereth

Achshaph

?Madon *Sea of Chinnereth*

Jokneam

Shimron

Dor

Megiddo

Beth-shan

Taanach

Canaanite forces gather at Waters of Merom

Canaanites pursued by Israelites

Israelite forces make surprise attack on Canaanites

Area of Israelite settlement

Part of the excavations of the ancient city of Jericho.

Part of the excavations at Hazor, north of Galilee, the largest city in Canaan during the period of the Israelite invasion.

The captured territories were allocated by lot to the Israelite tribes as their inheritance (Joshua 13–22). The Israelites gradually took control of the highlands, and tended to settle there. The Canaanites, with their superior weaponry, especially the iron chariot, continued to prevail in the lowland areas. The Israelites did not yet possess the ability to smelt iron. Thus, when the land was divided among the tribes of Israel, some towns remained unconquered, and the Israelites had to live alongside the Canaanites.

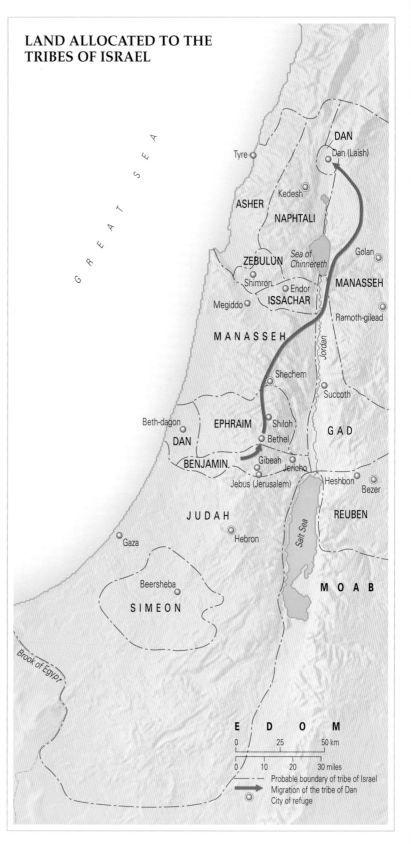

LAND ALLOCATED TO THE TRIBES OF ISRAEL

GREAT SEA

DAN
Tyre
Dan (Laish)
Kedesh
ASHER
NAPHTALI
ZEBULUN
Sea of Chinnereth
Golan
Shimron
Endor
MANASSEH
Megiddo
ISSACHAR
Ramoth-gilead
MANASSEH
Jordan
Shechem
Succoth
Beth-dagon
EPHRAIM
Shiloh
GAD
DAN
Bethel
BENJAMIN
Gibeah
Jebus (Jerusalem)
Jericho
Heshbon
Bezer
JUDAH
REUBEN
Gaza
Hebron
Salt Sea
MOAB
Beersheba
SIMEON
Brook of Egypt
E D O M

0   25   50 km
0   10   20   30 miles

— · — Probable boundary of tribe of Israel
→ Migration of the tribe of Dan
○ City of refuge

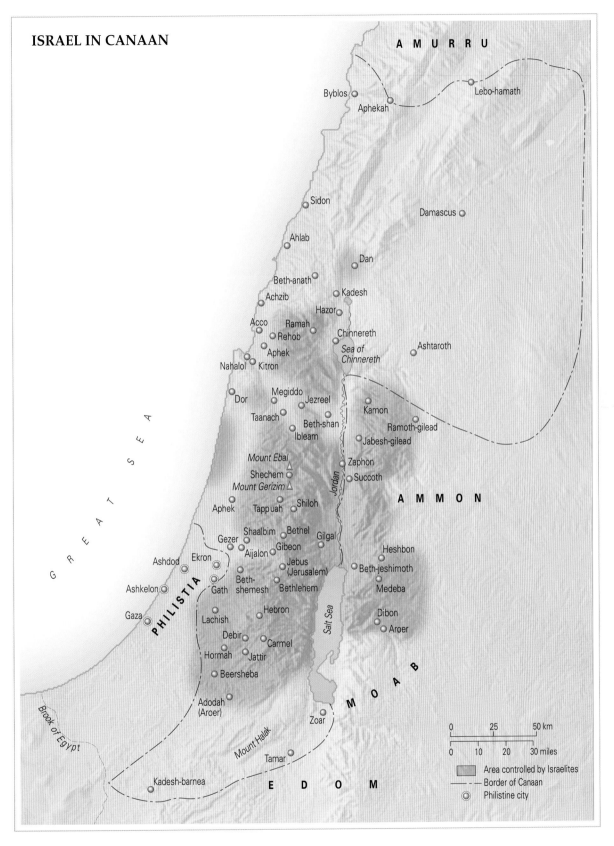

ISRAEL IN CANAAN

AMURRU

Byblos
Aphekah
Lebo-hamath

Sidon
Damascus

Ahlab

Dan

Beth-anath
Kadesh
Achzib
Hazor
Acco Ramah
Rehob Chinnereth Ashtaroth
Aphek *Sea of*
Nahalol Kitron *Chinnereth*

Dor Megiddo
Jezreel
Kamon
Taanach Ramoth-gilead
Beth-shan
Ibleam Jabesh-gilead

Mount Ebal Zaphon
Shechem Succoth
Mount Gerizim
Aphek Tappuah Shiloh AMMON

Shaalbim Bethel
Gezer Gilgal Heshbon
Aijalon Gibeon
Ashdod Ekron Jebus Beth-jeshimoth
(Jerusalem)
Ashkelon Beth- Bethlehem Medeba
Gath shemesh

Gaza Hebron Dibon
Lachish Aroer
Debir
Hormah Carmel
Jattir

Beersheba

PHILISTIA

Salt Sea

MOAB

Adodah
(Aroer)
Zoar

Brook of Egypt

Mount Halak
Tamar

Kadesh-barnea E D O M

G R E A T S E A

Jordan

0		25		50 km
0	10	20	30 miles	

Area controlled by Israelites
— ·— Border of Canaan
◎ Philistine city

THE JUDGES

Although the children of Israel were now settled in the land that God had promised to give them, they had not removed all its former inhabitants, as we have seen. Heathen culture persisted within her territories and penetrated her beliefs. This situation continued throughout the period of some 200 years described in the Book of Judges. A cycle of back-sliding, oppression, and deliverance kept repeating itself. First back-sliding—worshiping gods of the surrounding peoples; then judg-ment—in the form of foreign op-pression; finally deliverance—as the Lord raised up judges. Yet the people of Israel would not listen to their judges, but turned to other gods again (Judges 2:11–17).

The judges combined several functions. Primarily, they were military leaders, appointed to de-liver Israel from her enemies. Othniel rescued Israel from Aram (Judges 3:7–11) and Ehud delivered Israel from the Moabites (Judges 3:12–30). Deborah the prophet, with

The hills west of Hebron, in the territory disputed with the Philistines in the time of the judges.

Barak, a leader from the tribe of Naphtali, delivered the Israelites from oppression by the Canaanites led by King Jabin of Hazor in the north (Judges 4–5). When Sisera, Jabin's general, brought his infantry and 900 iron chariots to the foot of Mount Tabor, Barak stationed his forces on the mountain, and then swept down on Sisera's troops, with

devastating effect, pursuing the defeated enemy across country.

Israel was also threatened by the Midianites, a fierce desert tribe who used camels in their assaults. A reluctant general named Gideon delivered Israel from the Midianites, surprising them with a nighttime raid (Judges 6–7); while Jephthah rescued Israel from the Ammonites

The unmistakable profile of Mount Tabor, site of Deborah's famous victory over the Canaanite charioteers.

THE JUDGES

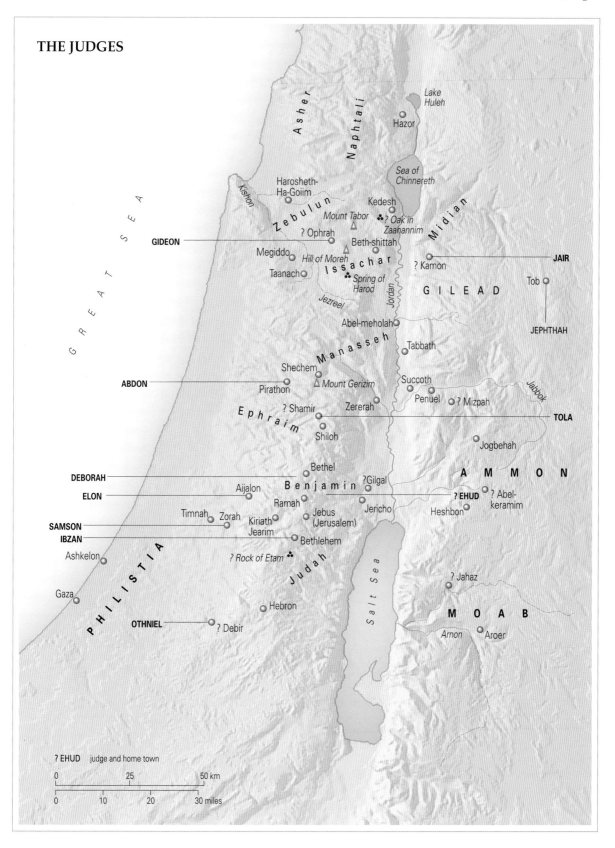

Asher

Naphtali

Lake Huleh

Hazor

Haaaroosheth-Ha-Goiim

Kishon

Sea of Chinnereth

Kedesh

Zebulun

Mount Tabor

? Oak in Zaanannim

Midian

? Ophrah

GIDEON

Beth-shittah

Megiddo

Hill of Moreh

I s s a c h a r

? Kamon

JAIR

Taanach

Spring of Harod

Jezreel

Jordan

G I L E A D

Tob

G R E A T   S E A

Abel-meholah

JEPHTHAH

Tabbath

M a n a s s e h

Shechem

ABDON

Pirathon

△ *Mount Gerizim*

Succoth

Penuel

? *Shamir*

Zererah

? Mizpah

E p h r a i m

TOLA

Shiloh

Jabbok

Jogbehah

Bethel

A M M O N

DEBORAH

?Gilgal

ELON

Aijalon

B e n j a m i n

Ramah

Jebus (Jerusalem)

Jericho

? EHUD

? Abel-keramim

Timnah

Zorah

SAMSON

Kiriath Jearim

Heshbon

IBZAN

Bethlehem

Ashkelon

? Rock of Etam

J u d a h

? Jahaz

Gaza

P H I L I S T I A

S a l t   S e a

M O A B

Hebron

OTHNIEL

? *Debir*

Arnon

Aroer

? EHUD   judge and home town

0   25   50 km

0   10   20   30 miles

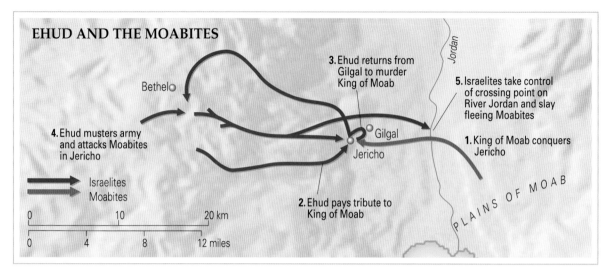

EHUD AND THE MOABITES

3. Ehud returns from Gilgal to murder King of Moab

5. Israelites take control of crossing point on River Jordan and slay fleeing Moabites

4. Ehud musters army and attacks Moabites in Jericho

Bethel

Gilgal

Jericho

1. King of Moab conquers Jericho

2. Ehud pays tribute to King of Moab

Israelites
Moabites

PLAINS OF MOAB

Jordan

0   10   20 km
0   4   8   12 miles

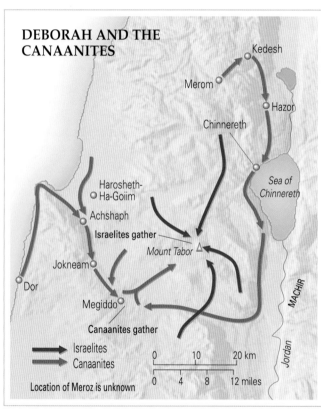

DEBORAH AND THE CANAANITES

Kedesh
Merom
Hazor
Chinnereth
Harosheth-Ha-Goiim
Achshaph
Sea of Chinnereth
Israelites gather
Mount Tabor
Jokneam
Dor
Megiddo
Canaanites gather

Israelites
Canaanites

Location of Meroz is unknown

MACHIR
Jordan

0   10   20 km
0   4   8   12 miles

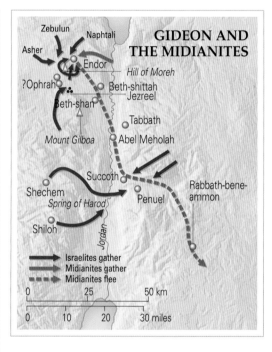

GIDEON AND THE MIDIANITES

Zebulun   Naphtali
Asher
Endor
Hill of Moreh
?Ophrah   Beth-shittah
Jezreel
Beth-shan   Tabbath
Mount Gilboa   Abel Meholah
Succoth
Shechem   Penuel   Rabbath-bene-ammon
Spring of Harod
Shiloh
Jordan

Israelites gather
Midianites gather
Midianites flee

0   25   50 km
0   10   20   30 miles

(Judges 10:6–11:33); and Samson from the Philistines (Judges 13–16).

The judges were also spiritual leaders, though not all were equally devoted to God. Finally, they were literally judges, hearing cases and administering justice in Israel.

The judges spanned the period from Joshua's settlement to the setting up of a monarchy. From time to time there were leagues of tribes (Judges 4:5; 6:35; 20:1), but there was little political unity between north and south—in fact there

seems to have been little law and order throughout this period, which is summed up by the last words of the book of Judges: "Everyone did as he thought best."

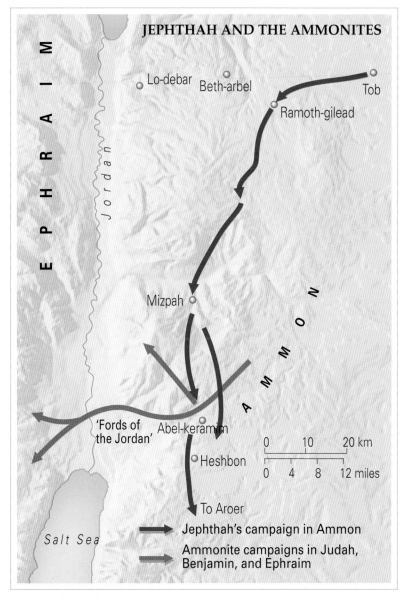

JEPHTHAH AND THE AMMONITES

E P H R A I M

Jordan

Lo-debar
Beth-arbel
Tob
Ramoth-gilead

A M M O N

Mizpah

'Fords of the Jordan'
Abel-keramim

0   10   20 km
0 4   8   12 miles

Heshbon

Salt Sea

To Aroer

→ Jephthah's campaign in Ammon
→ Ammonite campaigns in Judah, Benjamin, and Ephraim

Fields near Endor, site of Gideon's victory over the Midianites.

An Israelite archer.

Remains of the Chalcolithic temple (4000–3200 B.C.) at Megiddo, where the Canaanites mustered before facing Deborah on Mount Tabor.

31

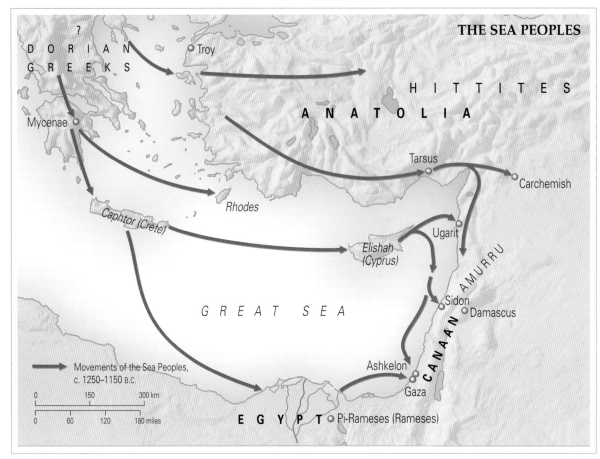

THE SEA PEOPLES

D O R I A N
G R E E K S

?

Troy

H I T T I T E S

A N A T O L I A

Mycenae

Tarsus

Carchemish

Rhodes

Caphtor (Crete)

Ugarit

Elishah
(Cyprus)

A M U R R U

G R E A T   S E A

Sidon
Damascus

C A N A A N

Ashkelon

Movements of the Sea Peoples,
c. 1250–1150 B.C.

Gaza

0   150   300 km

0   60   120   180 miles

E G Y P T   Pi-Rameses (Rameses)

THE PHILISTINES

Large numbers of "Sea Peoples," as the Egyptians called them, including the Philistines, migrated to the shores of the eastern Mediterranean between about 1250 B.C. and 1150 B.C. Rameses III records how he repelled their forces from the Nile Delta in 1174 B.C., after which they settled along the coast of the southern Levant (eastern Mediterranean), where they destroyed existing Canaanite cities and built their own.

Archaeological finds include distinctive Mycenaean-style pottery. Indications of a well-organized civilization support the Israelites' experience that the Philistines were powerful. Of Israel's judges, only Samson could achieve temporary success against them (Judges 13–16).

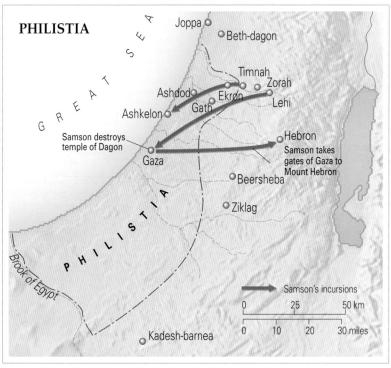

PHILISTIA

Joppa
Beth-dagon

G R E A T   S E A

Timnah
Zorah

Ashdod   Ekron
Lehi

Ashkelon   Gath

Samson destroys
temple of Dagon

Hebron
Samson takes
gates of Gaza to
Mount Hebron

Gaza

Beersheba

P H I L I S T I A

Ziklag

Brook of Egypt

Samson's incursions

0   25   50 km

0   10   20   30 miles

Kadesh-barnea

CAPTURE OF THE ARK

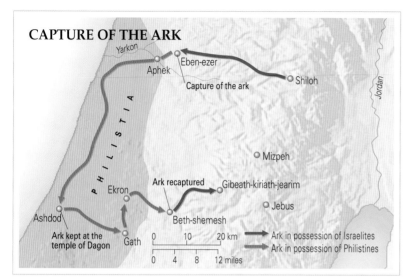

SAMUEL

The greatest of Israel's judges was Samuel. Dedicated to the Lord before his birth, Samuel was brought up at Shiloh under the high priest Eli. (While Eli was high priest, when Samuel was a mere child, the Philistines captured the Ark of the Covenant and took it from Shiloh to Ashdod.) To judge Israel, it was Samuel's custom to go on circuit every year from Ramah, his home-town, to Bethel, Gilgal, and Mizpah (1 Samuel 7:15–17). He relied on prayer rather than military prowess during his time as Israel's judge.

When Samuel grew old and appointed his sons as judges, they accepted bribes and perverted justice (1 Samuel 8:1–3). The elders of Israel demanded that Samuel appoint a king to govern them.

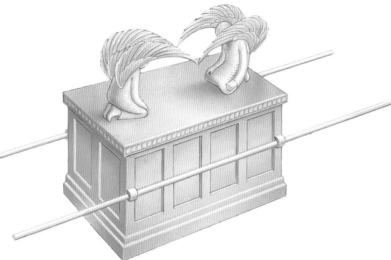

Left: **An artist's impression of the Ark of the Covenant, which was housed in the holy of holies within the tabernacle.**

Below: **Representation of a Phoenician warship, possibly similar to the vessels that carried the Philistines to the Holy Land.**

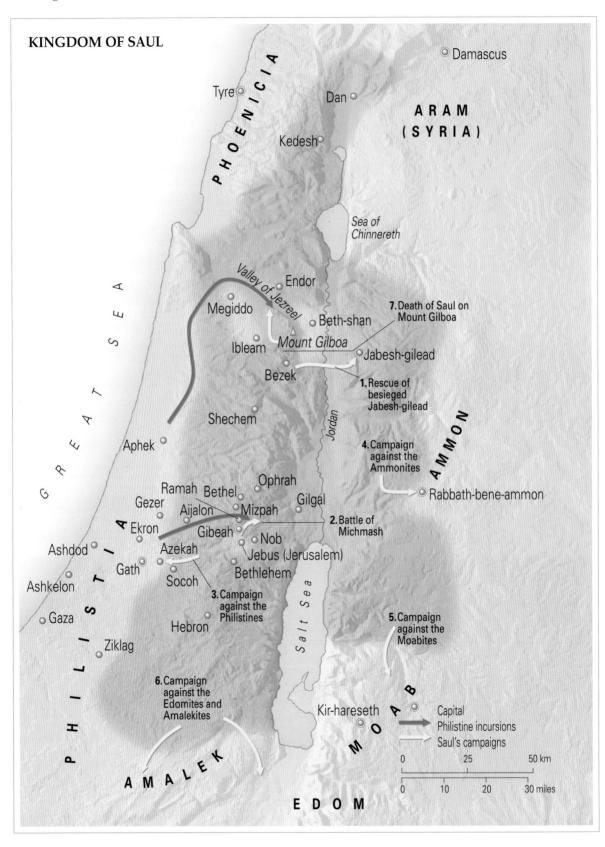

KINGDOM OF SAUL

Damascus

Tyre

PHOENICIA

Dan

Kedesh

ARAM
(SYRIA)

Sea of
Chinnereth

G R E A T   S E A

Valley of Jezreel

Endor

Megiddo

Beth-shan

7. Death of Saul on
Mount Gilboa

Ibleam

Mount Gilboa

Jabesh-gilead

Bezek

1. Rescue of
besieged
Jabesh-gilead

Shechem

Jordan

4. Campaign
against the
Ammonites

AMMON

Aphek

Ophrah

Ramah   Bethel

Gilgal

Rabbath-bene-ammon

Gezer   Aijalon   Mizpah

Ekron   Gibeah

2. Battle of
Michmash

Ashdod   Azekah

Nob

Jebus (Jerusalem)

Gath

Socoh

Bethlehem

Ashkelon

3. Campaign
against the
Philistines

S a l t   S e a

5. Campaign
against the
Moabites

Gaza

P H I L I S T I A

Ziklag

Hebron

6. Campaign
against the
Edomites and
Amalekites

Kir-hareseth

M O A B

Capital

Philistine incursions

Saul's campaigns

A M A L E K

0   25   50 km

E D O M

0   10   20   30 miles

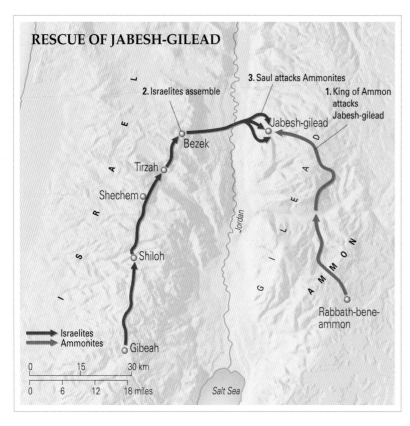

RESCUE OF JABESH-GILEAD

3. Saul attacks Ammonites

1. King of Ammon attacks Jabesh-gilead

2. Israelites assemble

Jabesh-gilead

Bezek

Tirzah

Shechem

Jordan

Shiloh

Rabbath-bene-ammon

I S R A E L

G I L E A D

A M M O N

→ Israelites
→ Ammonites

| 0 | 15 | 30 km |
| 0 | 6 | 12 | 18 miles |

Gibeah

Salt Sea

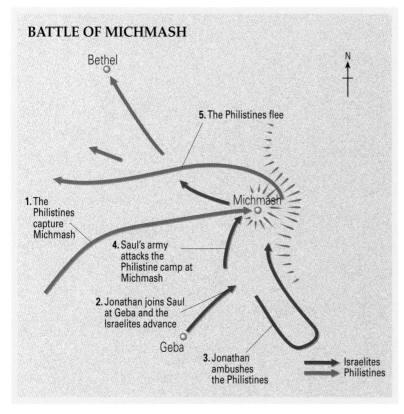

BATTLE OF MICHMASH

Bethel

N

5. The Philistines flee

1. The Philistines capture Michmash

Michmash

4. Saul's army attacks the Philistine camp at Michmash

2. Jonathan joins Saul at Geba and the Israelites advance

Geba

3. Jonathan ambushes the Philistines

→ Israelites
→ Philistines

THE KINGDOM OF SAUL

Saul was made king of Israel by the prophet Samuel in response to popular clamor for a king (1 Samuel 8:5). Neighboring states were kingdoms, and it was believed that Israel's military failures were due to her lack of leadership and unity.

Israel's first king began his reign with great promise. Saul was rich, tall, handsome, young, and popular. He led Israel successfully against the Ammonites in the relief of Jabesh-gilead, even before being anointed king at Gilgal. In a series of assaults on Philistine garrisons from Michmash to Aijalon, the Israelites marked up a number of victories over their old enemy (1 Samuel 14). With the help of his son Jonathan's audacious ambush tactics, Saul recorded a particularly notable victory at Michmash.

Successful campaigns to the south of the kingdom prepared the way for Saul's successor, David, to enlarge the realm. However, Saul's jealousy of David, to the point of trying to kill him, marks the turn in Saul's fortunes. He became enraged when he heard the women sing, "Saul has killed his thousands, David his tens of thousands." After consulting a witch at Endor, he and Jonathan died when the Israelites were defeated by the Philistines at the Battle of Gilboa (1 Samuel 31:1–6). David was overcome with grief: "Your glory, O Israel, lies slain upon your heights. How the mighty have fallen!" (2 Samuel 1:19).

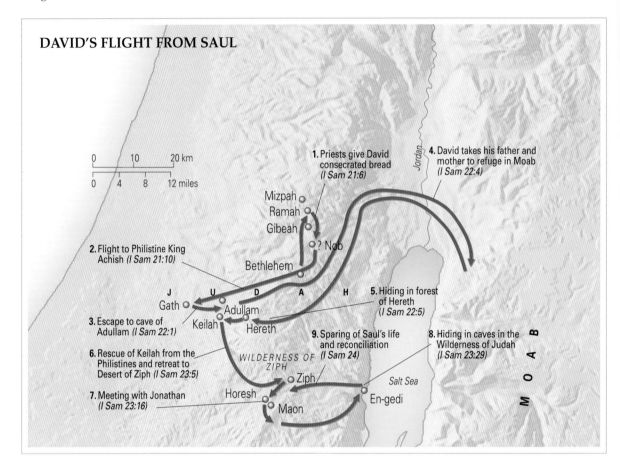

DAVID'S FLIGHT FROM SAUL

0   10   20 km
0   4   8   12 miles

1. Priests give David consecrated bread (*I Sam 21:6*)

4. David takes his father and mother to refuge in Moab (*I Sam 22:4*)

Jordan

Mizpah
Ramah
Gibeah
? Nob

2. Flight to Philistine King Achish (*I Sam 21:10*)

Bethlehem

J   U   D   A   H

Gath
Adullam
Keilah
Hereth

5. Hiding in forest of Hereth (*I Sam 22:5*)

3. Escape to cave of Adullam (*I Sam 22:1*)

9. Sparing of Saul's life and reconciliation (*I Sam 24*)

8. Hiding in caves in the Wilderness of Judah (*I Sam 23:29*)

6. Rescue of Keilah from the Philistines and retreat to Desert of Ziph (*I Sam 23:5*)

WILDERNESS OF ZIPH

Ziph
Horesh
Maon
En-gedi

Salt Sea

M O A B

7. Meeting with Jonathan (*I Sam 23:16*)

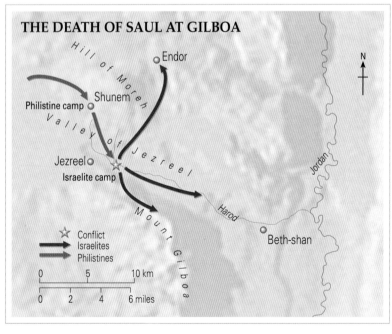

THE DEATH OF SAUL AT GILBOA

Hill of Moreh

Endor

Philistine camp
Shunem

Valley of Jezreel

Jezreel
Israelite camp

N

Mount Gilboa

Harod

Beth-shan

⭐ Conflict
→ Israelites
→ Philistines

0   5   10 km
0   2   4   6 miles

KING DAVID

David had already been declared heir to the throne during Saul's lifetime, but spent the final years of Saul's reign in flight from his jealousy. David sought refuge in many places, including the court of a Philistine king.

David began his own reign in Hebron, where the men of his tribe, Judah, anointed him king. Seven years later, representatives of all the tribes of Israel came to Hebron, and he was anointed king a second time (2 Samuel 2–5). He moved his capital to Jebus (only now captured from the Jebusites), and changed its name to Jerusalem, "city of peace." The Ark of the Covenant (the chest from the tabernacle containing the sacred tablets of Moses) was ceremoniously brought to the city (2 Samuel 6).

DAVID'S CAPTURE OF JERUSALEM (JEBUS)

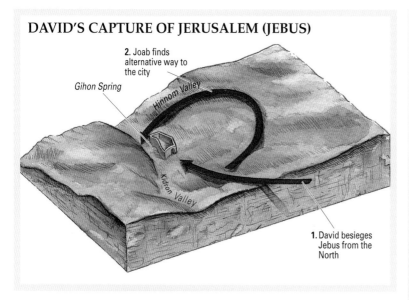

2. Joab finds alternative way to the city

Gihon Spring

Hinnom Valley

Kidron Valley

1. David besieges Jebus from the North

CROSS-SECTION THROUGH GIHON SPRING

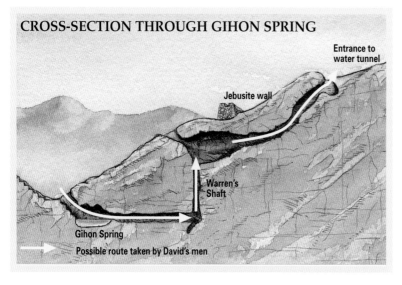

Entrance to water tunnel

Jebusite wall

Warren's Shaft

Gihon Spring

Possible route taken by David's men

Above: Remains of the Jebusite defensive wall of Jerusalem, now situated just outside the old city of Jerusalem.

Left: The Gihon spring flows through the Kidron Valley and was the main source of water for ancient Jerusalem. It is thought that David captured the city by making a surprise attack via the Gihon spring. The cross-section shows the possible route referred to in 2 Samuel 5:8, "Whoever conquers the Jebusites will have to use the water shaft. . . ."

JERUSALEM AT THE TIME OF DAVID

David's capture of Jerusalem completed the conquest of Canaan. The Jebusite city that David captured was built on a spur of a hill to the north. Apart from its good defensive position, with high surrounding walls, this site was also chosen for its water supply, the Gihon spring, which lay at the foot of the eastern slope and flowed through the Kidron Valley. It is thought that David actually cap-

tured the city by making a surprise attack via the Gihon spring.

There was limited space on this site, and many houses had to be built on stone terraces on the slopes. As the city expanded in Solomon's time, so the center shifted northward to the flatter top of the hill. David selected an old Jebusite threshing floor, reputedly the site of Isaac's sacrifice on Mount Moriah, as the place for the altar (2 Samuel 24:18), and it was here that Solomon built his temple.

Having built a palace for himself in Jerusalem, David was keen to build a house for the Lord. But the prophet Nathan forbade it, telling him his son would be allowed to build the temple (2 Samuel 7:11–16).

There are two reasons why David could not build the temple: he was being arrogant (thinking he was doing God a favor), and he had shed too much blood.

DAVID'S UNITED KINGDOM

David now set about consolidating what Saul had started: uniting his people, breaking the power of the Philistines, and expanding the frontiers of his kingdom over the Edomites, Ammonites, Moabites, and Arameans.

David's first achievement was to make the country safe from her enemies. David extended his kingdom to include lands from Dan to the Brook of Egypt. His empire stretched much farther, to the Euphrates in the north and Ezion-geber on the Gulf of Aqaba in the south, while the peoples of Edom, Moab, Ammon, and Aram became his vassal states and were forced to pay tribute (2 Samuel 8:2–14). This, together with the tax levied on the huge volume of trade that passed through the Levant, brought in a healthy income for the treasury.

David was able to commission new buildings, such as his own palace in Jerusalem, for which he used craftsmen from neighboring states (2 Samuel 5:11). The king was careful to maintain peace treaties with his allies, the Philistines, and the people of Hamath. In view of his extensive conquests it was galling for him to suffer rebellion at home, from his son Absalom and from a pretender named Sheba, the Benjaminite. However, David and his generals managed to hold together the hegemony they had imposed on the Levant, despite these two rebellions.

At his death, c. 970 B.C., David handed over to his son Solomon an empire that fifty years earlier would have been unimaginable, and the size of which would not be seen again under Israelite rule. It was said to extend from river (the Euphrates) to river (the Nile). But David was far from being a mere warlord. He was a poet and musician, who had often soothed Saul's depression with his lyre; magnanimous to his enemies and loyal to his friends. Israel never forgot God's covenant with David; the Israelites believed that when the Messiah came, He would be a Son of David.

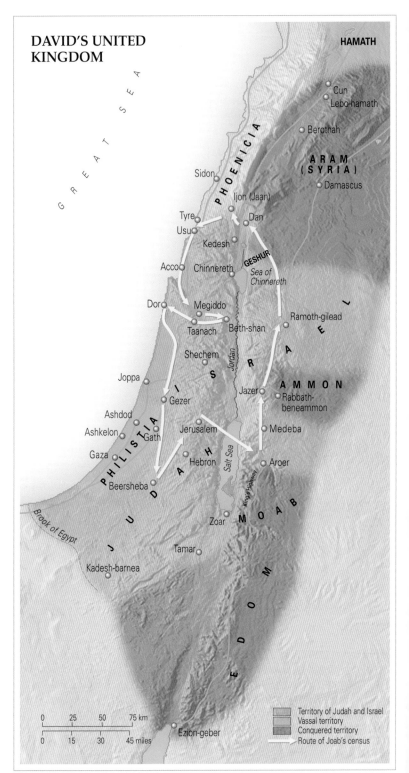

DAVID'S UNITED KINGDOM

HAMATH

Cun
Lebo-hamath

Berothah

A R A M (S Y R I A)

Damascus

Sidon

G R E A T   S E A

PHOENICIA

Ijon (Jaan)

Tyre
Usu

Dan

Kedesh

GESHUR

Acco

Chinnereth

Sea of Chinnereth

Dor

Megiddo

Ramoth-gilead

Taanach

Beth-shan

I S R A E L

Shechem

Jordan

Joppa

Jazer

A M M O N

Gezer

Rabbath-beneammon

Ashdod
Ashkelon

Gath

Jerusalem

Medeba

Gaza

P H I L I S T I A

J U D A H

Hebron

Salt Sea

Aroer

Beersheba

King's Highway

M O A B

Zoar

Brook of Egypt

J U D A H

Tamar

E D O M

Kadesh-barnea

| 0 | 25 | 50 | 75 km |
| 0 | 15 | 30 | 45 miles |

Ezion-geber

Territory of Judah and Israel
Vassal territory
Conquered territory
Route of Joab's census

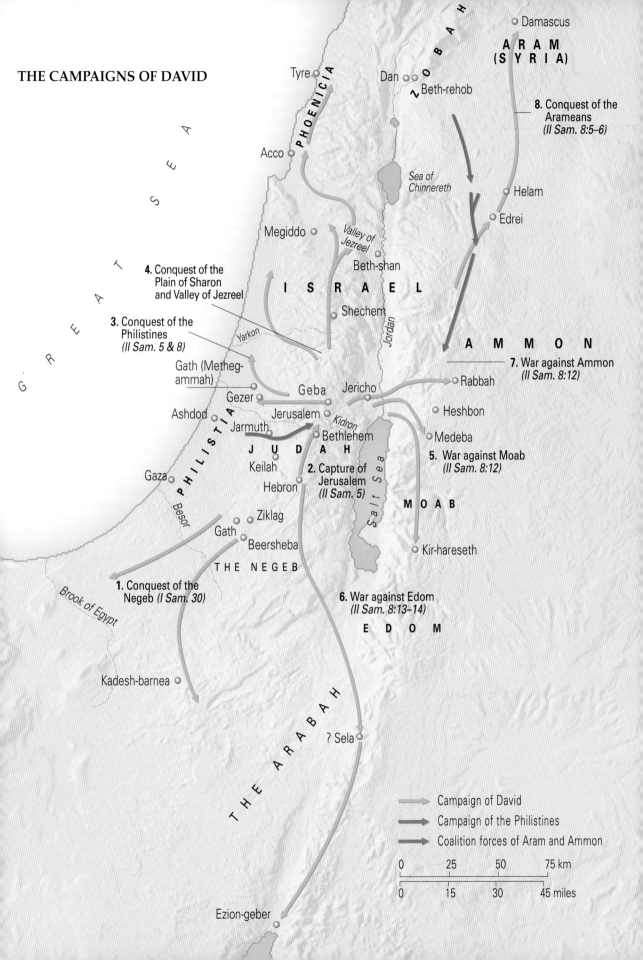

THE CAMPAIGNS OF DAVID

Damascus

ARAM (SYRIA)

Tyre

Dan

Beth-rehob

ZOBAH

PHOENICIA

8. Conquest of the
Arameans
(II Sam. 8:5–6)

Acco

Sea of
Chinnereth

Helam

Edrei

Megiddo

Valley of
Jezreel

Beth-shan

G R E A T   S E A

4. Conquest of the
Plain of Sharon
and Valley of Jezreel

I S R A E L

Shechem

Jordan

3. Conquest of the
Philistines
(II Sam. 5 & 8)

Yarkon

A M M O N

7. War against Ammon
(II Sam. 8:12)

Gath (Metheg-
ammah)

Geba

Jericho

Rabbah

Gezer

Jerusalem

Heshbon

Ashdod

Kidron

Jarmuth

Bethlehem

Medeba

J U D A H

Keilah

2. Capture of
Jerusalem
(II Sam. 5)

5. War against Moab
(II Sam. 8:12)

Gaza

Hebron

Salt Sea

M O A B

Besor

Ziklag

Gath

Beersheba

Kir-hareseth

T H E   N E G E B

1. Conquest of the
Negeb (I Sam. 30)

6. War against Edom
(II Sam. 8:13–14)

E D O M

Brook of Egypt

Kadesh-barnea

T H E   A R A B A H

? Sela

Campaign of David

Campaign of the Philistines

Coalition forces of Aram and Ammon

0   25   50   75 km

0   15   30   45 miles

Ezion-geber

SOLOMON'S UNITED KINGDOM

After winning a difficult succession struggle, Solomon reigned for some forty years (c. 970–930 B.C.). During his reign, the kingdom of Israel reached its peak of magnificence. Solomon's strengths were administration, public works, and diplomacy. Soon after his accession to the throne he prayed that God would give him wisdom (1 Kings 3:9) and his prayer was answered.

Solomon married the daughters of neighboring kings as a means of sealing diplomatic relations and entered joint commercial enterprises with Hiram, the king of the Phoenician city of Tyre. He divided his kingdom into twelve administrative districts (1 Kings 4:7–19) under twelve officers responsible for providing for the royal household, one each month of the year. This facilitated a nationwide building program. Each district administrator was responsible for organizing the forced labor (corvée) of 30,000 men needed to quarry the hill country and produce masonry for building.

Solomon built palaces for himself and his queen in Jerusalem; halls of assembly, justice, and arms; and the great temple, made of stone, cedar, cypress, and gold. He built even pagan temples so that his foreign wives could worship their gods. His reputation for splendor, wisdom, and justice spread far, and under his rule his people enjoyed peace and prosperity (1 Kings 4:20, 25). However, the extravagance of some of Solomon's schemes and the forced-labor policy sowed the seeds of discontent, which resulted in the breakup of the kingdom during his successor's reign.

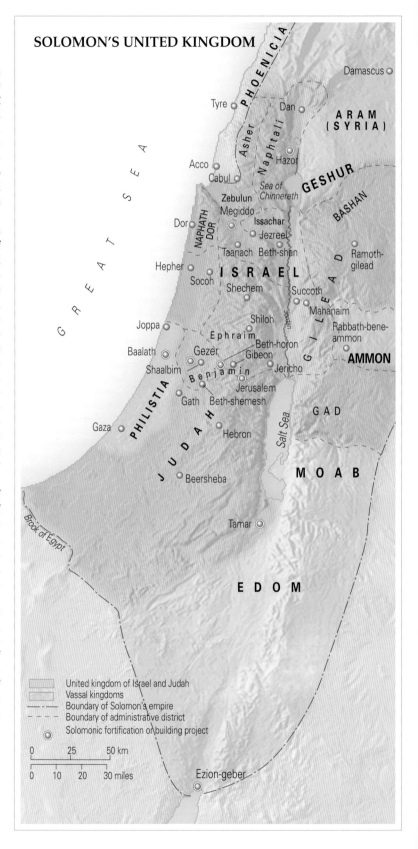

SOLOMON'S UNITED KINGDOM

United kingdom of Israel and Judah
Vassal kingdoms
Boundary of Solomon's empire
Boundary of administrative district
Solomonic fortification or building project

0   25   50 km
0 10 20 30 miles

MEGIDDO

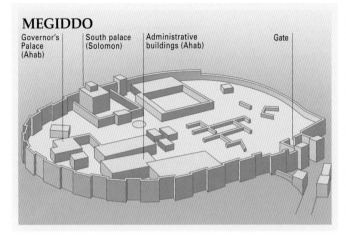

Governor's Palace (Ahab) | South palace (Solomon) | Administrative buildings (Ahab) | Gate

JERUSALEM IN THE TIME OF DAVID AND SOLOMON

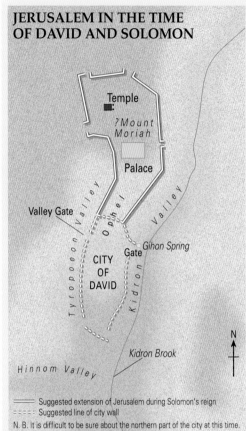

Temple

?Mount Moriah

Palace

Valley Gate

Tyropoeon Valley

Ophel

Kidron Valley

Gate   Gihon Spring

CITY OF DAVID

Kidron Brook

Hinnom Valley

N

———— Suggested extension of Jerusalem during Solomon's reign
- - - - - Suggested line of city wall
N. B. It is difficult to be sure about the northern part of the city at this time.

SOLOMON'S TEMPLE

Nothing now remains of Solomon's temple. It is described in detail in both 1 Kings and 2 Chronicles, where measurements are given and materials specified. Canaanite temple ruins have been excavated that are similar in style to the Biblical description and may have provided a prototype for Solomon's temple. The reconstruction illustrated shows three main chambers —a porch, a main hall, and the holy of holies. The chief priest's ritual duties were performed in the main hall, while the holy of holies housed the Ark of the Covenant, guarded by two cherubim.

Above: **Solomon fortified the gateway of the Canaanite city of Megiddo.**

Artist's cutaway impression of Solomon's temple, according to the description given in the Bible.

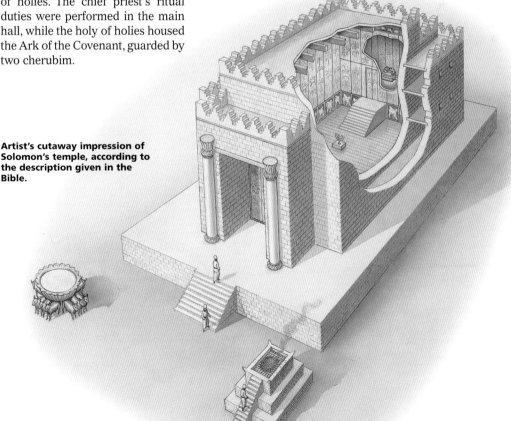

41

SOLOMON'S TRADING EMPIRE

Solomon developed a trade monopoly and exploited the natural resources of his empire. He fortified the cities of Hazor, Megiddo, Gezer, Lower Beth-horon, Baalath, and Tamar in the Arabah (1 Kings 6–7; 9:15–19). He built smelting furnaces for his iron- and copper-mining enterprises, and made a naval base at Ezion-geber. He raised a standing army, equipping himself with 1,400 chariots and 40,000 warhorses. He also founded Israel's navy, whose ships, kept in the Gulf of Aqaba, set out on distant trading voyages.

The two most lucrative trade routes in the Ancient Near East were the Way of the Sea, which linked Egypt with Asia, and the King's Highway, the main caravan route up from southern Arabia. At the time of the empire of David and Solomon, both of these routes were controlled by Israel. Solomon also controlled the maritime trade in a joint venture with King Hiram of Tyre: Hiram operated a coastal trade from Asia Minor that linked up with sea lanes from Ezion-geber to the Red Sea.

Merchant ships would leave Ezion-geber with cargo, such as wheat and olive oil, and sail to Ophir (thought to be present-day Somalia) and possibly on to India. They would return with gold, silver, ivory, and fine woods and exotic creatures (1 Kings 10:11, 22). A flourishing spice trade operated between Israel and southern Arabia, usually believed to be Sheba. The Queen of Sheba's liaison with Solomon is thought to have had a strong commercial interest.

THE DIVISION OF THE KINGDOM

At Solomon's death, c. 930 B.C., his son Rehoboam was recognized as the new king in Judah, but was rejected by the elders of the northern tribes at the Council of Shechem because of his father's repressive measures. Rehoboam, who had lived in exile in Egypt, refused to abandon similar measures. The northern tribes now elected the exiled Jeroboam as their leader. Two kingdoms emerged, Israel in the north and Judah in the south, divided approximately along the traditional boundary between Ephraim and Benjamin (1 Kings 12–13).

Saul, David, and Solomon had reigned over all Israel for forty years each, so that for the 120 years from approximately 1050–930 B.C. there had been a united kingdom. The new Northern Kingdom of Israel, with Jeroboam its first king, had as its capital city Shechem (later changed to Samaria). The Southern Kingdom of Judah, with Rehoboam its first king, had Jerusalem as its capital.

Israel had several changes of dynasty and lasted just over 200 years, until the destruction of Samaria in 722 B.C. Judah was more stable, retaining the dynasty of David throughout its longer history of about 350 years, until Jerusalem was also destroyed in 586 B.C.

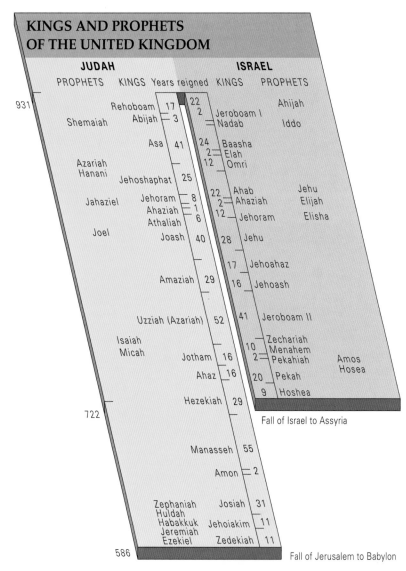

KINGS AND PROPHETS OF THE UNITED KINGDOM

JUDAH			ISRAEL	
PROPHETS	KINGS	Years reigned	KINGS	PROPHETS
			22	Ahijah
	Rehoboam	17	Jeroboam I	
Shemaiah	Abijah	3	2 Nadab	Iddo
	Asa	41	24 Baasha	
			2 Elah	
Azariah			12 Omri	
Hanani	Jehoshaphat	25		
			22 Ahab	Jehu
Jahaziel	Jehoram	8	2 Ahaziah	Elijah
	Ahaziah	1	12 Jehoram	Elisha
	Athaliah	6		
Joel	Joash	40	28 Jehu	
			17 Jehoahaz	
	Amaziah	29	16 Jehoash	
	Uzziah (Azariah)	52	41 Jeroboam II	
Isaiah			Zechariah	
Micah			10 Menahem	
	Jotham	16	2 Pekahiah	Amos
	Ahaz	16	20 Pekah	Hosea
			9 Hoshea	
	Hezekiah	29		

931

722

Fall of Israel to Assyria

	Manasseh	55		
	Amon	2		
Zephaniah	Josiah	31		
Huldah				
Habakkuk	Jehoiakim	11		
Jeremiah				
Ezekiel	Zedekiah	11		

586

Fall of Jerusalem to Babylon

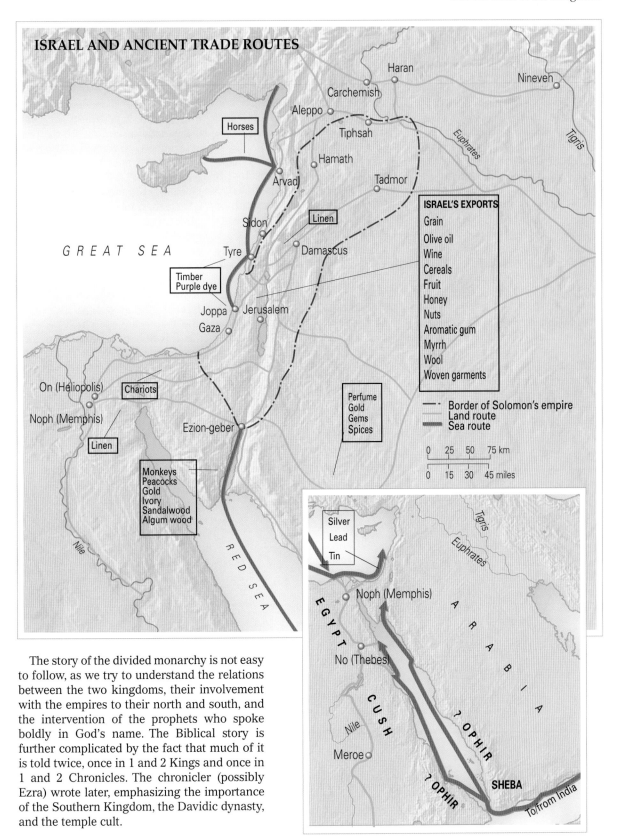

ISRAEL AND ANCIENT TRADE ROUTES

Horses

Linen

ISRAEL'S EXPORTS
Grain
Olive oil
Wine
Cereals
Fruit
Honey
Nuts
Aromatic gum
Myrrh
Wool
Woven garments

Timber
Purple dye

Perfume
Gold
Gems
Spices

— · — Border of Solomon's empire
Land route
Sea route

0   25   50   75 km
0   15   30   45 miles

Chariots

Linen

Monkeys
Peacocks
Gold
Ivory
Sandalwood
Algum wood

Silver
Lead
Tin

Haran
Carchemish
Nineveh
Aleppo
Tiphsah
Hamath
Tadmor
Euphrates
Tigris
Arvad
Sidon
Tyre
Damascus
GREAT SEA
Joppa Jerusalem
Gaza
On (Heliopolis)
Noph (Memphis)
Ezion-geber
Nile
RED SEA
Noph (Memphis)
No (Thebes)
EGYPT
CUSH
Nile
Meroe
ARABIA
OPHIR
OPHIR
SHEBA
To/from India
Tigris
Euphrates

The story of the divided monarchy is not easy to follow, as we try to understand the relations between the two kingdoms, their involvement with the empires to their north and south, and the intervention of the prophets who spoke boldly in God's name. The Biblical story is further complicated by the fact that much of it is told twice, once in 1 and 2 Kings and once in 1 and 2 Chronicles. The chronicler (possibly Ezra) wrote later, emphasizing the importance of the Southern Kingdom, the Davidic dynasty, and the temple cult.

PHARAOH SHISHAK INVADES

Conquered states broke away as civil war and diminishing control over trade routes weakened both kingdoms. Syria, Ammon, Moab, and the Philistines all reasserted their independence. Egypt, which for a long time had been unable to pursue her imperial ambitions into Asia, now took advantage of the situation and Pharaoh Shishak invaded Judah in the fifth year of Rehoboam's reign. This was followed up by a campaign in Israel, in spite of the pharaoh's sheltering Jeroboam during his earlier exile.

The invasion is recorded in the temple at Karnak, in Egypt. More than 150 places were captured by the Egyptians in Judah, the Negeb, Israel, and Transjordan. The speed and ferocity of Shishak's onslaught forced Rehoboam to surrender at Gibeon in order to prevent the destruction of Jerusalem. Shishak turned north and conquered Israel just as easily, Solomon's fortifications proving ineffective. One town after another was burned, including the stronghold of Megiddo.

An Egyptian warrior.

ISRAEL, THE NORTHERN KINGDOM

Jeroboam, the first ruler of the Northern Kingdom, had been one of Solomon's servants. Solomon had such a high opinion of Jeroboam's ability that he had put him in charge of the forced-labor levy. Later, Solomon came to suspect Jeroboam of treason, and the latter fled for his life to Egypt where he was sheltered by Shishak. Jeroboam only returned after Solomon's death to challenge Rehoboam, as we have seen.

In order to turn his people away from the house of David, Jeroboam determined to stop them from going on pilgrimage to Jerusalem. So he set up two alternative sanctuaries, one in the north, at Dan; the other in the south, at Bethel. He installed a golden calf in each place, and said: "Here are your gods . . . who brought you from Egypt" (1 Kings 12:28). For this reason Jeroboam is recorded as the one "who made Israel sin."

Jeroboam was succeeded on the throne of Israel by five kings of whom we know little. But in 881 B.C., some twenty-eight years after Jeroboam's death, and some fifty years after the separation of Israel from Judah, the dynasty of Omri began. Omri established his capital in Samaria, and made it almost impregnable, on a well-fortified hill. A period of relative peace and prosperity began. But Omri brought trouble to Israel by marrying his son Ahab (who succeeded him) to the Phoenician princess Jezebel, daughter of the king of Tyre. As a result Israel came under the influence of Phoenician culture, including the cult of Baal. For Jezebel not only worshiped Melqart (the main deity of Tyre—"Baal" in the Bible) herself, but maintained prophets of Baal at court, and involved her husband Ahab in her idolatry. She killed the prophets of God.

Israelite remains at Samaria, capital of the Northern Kingdom.

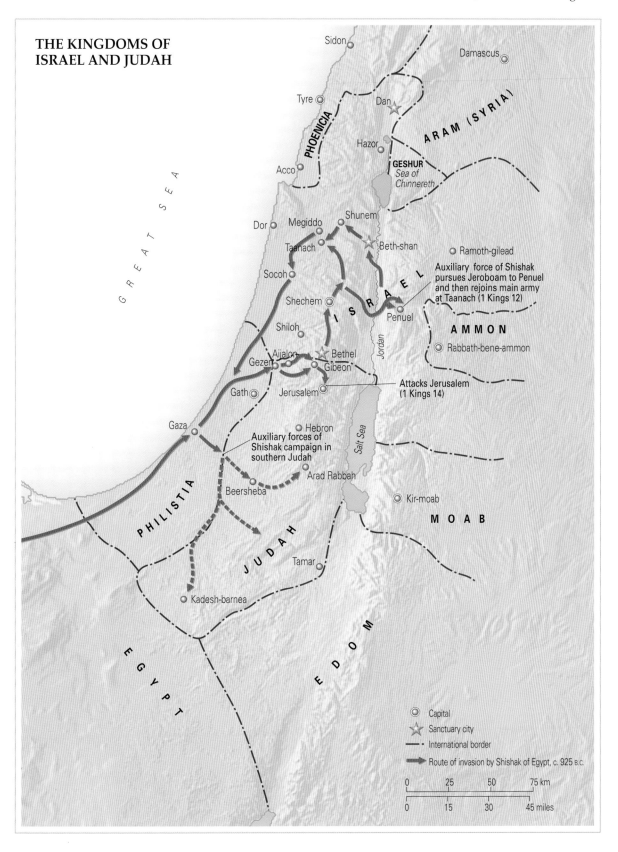

THE KINGDOMS OF ISRAEL AND JUDAH

Sidon

Damascus

Tyre

Dan

ARAM (SYRIA)

PHOENICIA

Hazor

GESHUR
Sea of Chinnereth

Acco

GREAT SEA

Dor

Megiddo

Shunem

Taanach

Beth-shan

Ramoth-gilead

Socoh

Auxiliary force of Shishak
pursues Jeroboam to Penuel
and then rejoins main army
at Taanach (1 Kings 12)

Shechem

ISRAEL

Penuel

AMMON

Shiloh

Jordan

Aijalon

Bethel

Rabbath-bene-ammon

Gezer

Gibeon

Gath

Jerusalem

Attacks Jerusalem
(1 Kings 14)

Gaza

Hebron

Auxiliary forces of
Shishak campaign in
southern Judah

Salt Sea

Beersheba

Arad Rabbah

Kir-moab

PHILISTIA

MOAB

JUDAH

Tamar

Kadesh-barnea

EGYPT

EDOM

◎ Capital

☆ Sanctuary city

–·– International border

➤ Route of invasion by Shishak of Egypt, c. 925 B.C.

| 0 | 25 | 50 | 75 km |

| 0 | 15 | 30 | 45 miles |

Statue of the prophet Elijah on Mount Carmel smiting the prophets of Baal.

A view from the steep slopes of Mount Carmel, site of Elijah's contest with the prophets of Baal.

ELIJAH AND ELISHA

Jezebel's sponsorship of Baal worship invoked the wrath of Israel's prophets, in particular Elijah (1 Kings 18). Prophets such as Elijah were to play a significant role in both Israel and Judah for the next 300 years. Elijah came from Gilead in Transjordan. Ascetic in lifestyle and fearless in his ministry, he denounced Ahab for troubling Israel by his religious defection. Elijah challenged the prophets of Baal to a contest on Mount Carmel, taunting the Israelites with wavering between two religions (1 Kings 18:21). When Baal's prophets failed to elicit a response from their god, Elijah prayed to Yahweh and fire from heaven ignited his sacrifice, thus showing that Yahweh was the true source of rain and fertility for the land.

Elijah knew that God was also angry with the king's oppression of his subjects. Next to one of Ahab's palaces on the Plain of Jezreel was a vineyard owned by a man named Naboth. Ahab coveted it, but Naboth refused to sell his father's inheritance. So Queen Jezebel had Naboth assassinated and his property annexed for her husband. Elijah challenged the king, whom he met in the vineyard (1 Kings 21:17–20).

Naboth's innocent blood was avenged by Jehu, an Israelite general, who was now anointed king on the authority of the prophet Elisha. Elisha succeeded Elijah and continued Elijah's policies. By his support for Jehu, he brought about the downfall of the dynasty of Omri. Jehu liquidated the house of Ahab and rid the land of Baalism.

Drawing of a relief depicting the pagan deity Baal.

46

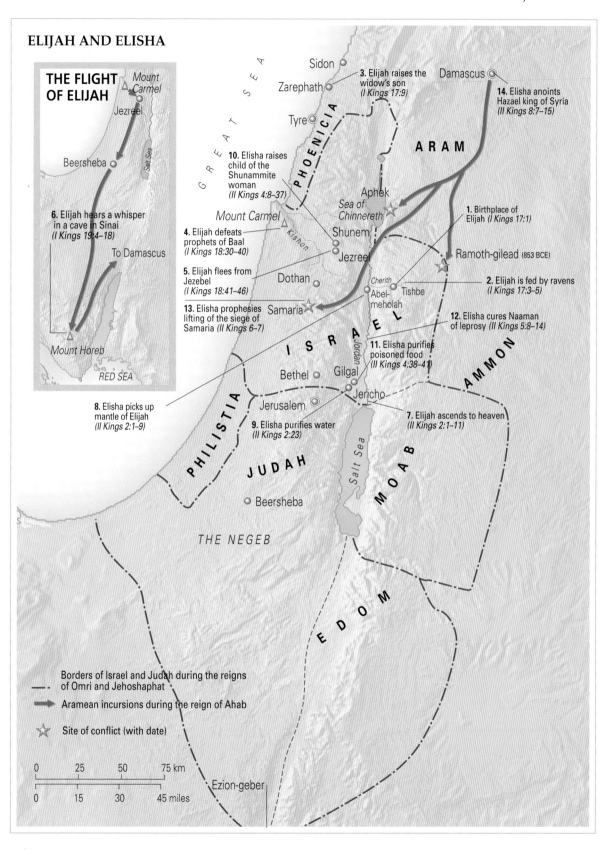

ELIJAH AND ELISHA

THE FLIGHT OF ELIJAH

Mount Carmel

Jezreel

Beersheba

Salt Sea

6. Elijah hears a whisper in a cave in Sinai (I Kings 19:4–18)

To Damascus

Mount Horeb

RED SEA

8. Elisha picks up mantle of Elijah (II Kings 2:1–9)

GREAT SEA

Sidon

Zarephath

Tyre

PHOENICIA

3. Elijah raises the widow's son (I Kings 17:9)

Damascus

14. Elisha anoints Hazael king of Syria (II Kings 8:7–15)

ARAM

10. Elisha raises child of the Shunammite woman (II Kings 4:8–37)

Aphek

Sea of Chinnereth

Mount Carmel

Shunem

4. Elijah defeats prophets of Baal (I Kings 18:30–40)

Kishon

Jezreel

5. Elijah flees from Jezebel (I Kings 18:41–46)

Dothan

Cherith

Abel-meholah

Tishbe

1. Birthplace of Elijah (I Kings 17:1)

Ramoth-gilead (853 BCE)

2. Elijah is fed by ravens (I Kings 17:3–5)

12. Elisha cures Naaman of leprosy (II Kings 5:8–14)

13. Elisha prophesies lifting of the siege of Samaria (II Kings 6–7)

Samaria

ISRAEL

Jordan

11. Elisha purifies poisoned food (II Kings 4:38–41)

AMMON

Bethel

Gilgal

Jericho

Jerusalem

9. Elisha purifies water (II Kings 2:23)

PHILISTIA

JUDAH

Beersheba

THE NEGEB

Salt Sea

7. Elijah ascends to heaven (II Kings 2:1–11)

MOAB

EDOM

Borders of Israel and Judah during the reigns of Omri and Jehoshaphat

Aramean incursions during the reign of Ahab

Site of conflict (with date)

0 25 50 75 km
0 15 30 45 miles

Ezion-geber

47

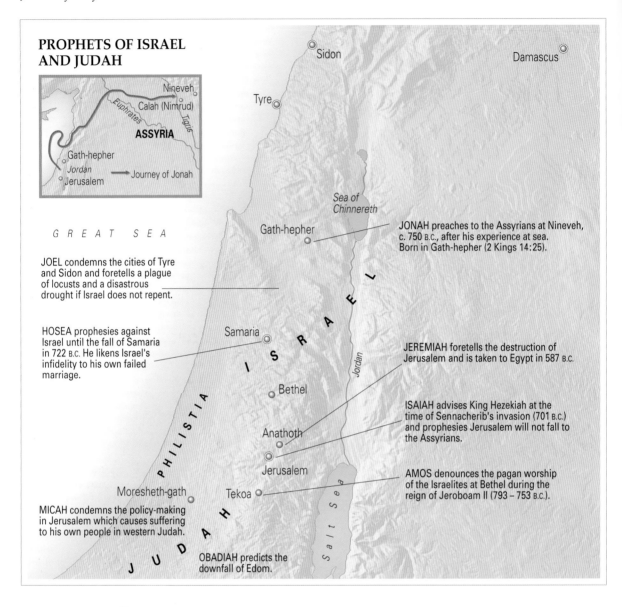

PROPHETS OF ISRAEL AND JUDAH

ASSYRIA

Journey of Jonah

GREAT SEA

JONAH preaches to the Assyrians at Nineveh, c. 750 B.C., after his experience at sea. Born in Gath-hepher (2 Kings 14:25).

JOEL condemns the cities of Tyre and Sidon and foretells a plague of locusts and a disastrous drought if Israel does not repent.

HOSEA prophesies against Israel until the fall of Samaria in 722 B.C. He likens Israel's infidelity to his own failed marriage.

JEREMIAH foretells the destruction of Jerusalem and is taken to Egypt in 587 B.C.

ISAIAH advises King Hezekiah at the time of Sennacherib's invasion (701 B.C.) and prophesies Jerusalem will not fall to the Assyrians.

AMOS denounces the pagan worship of the Israelites at Bethel during the reign of Jeroboam II (793 – 753 B.C.).

MICAH condemns the policy-making in Jerusalem which causes suffering to his own people in western Judah.

OBADIAH predicts the downfall of Edom.

JEHU'S DYNASTY

The dynasty of Jehu lasted nearly a hundred years (c. 841–753 B.C.), almost half the total duration of the Northern Kingdom. During the early years there was almost continuous war with Syria, which won the entire Transjordan from Jehu. But his grandson began to recover these territories, and his great-grandson Jeroboam II completed the process.

Israel and Judah became powerful and wealthy nations during the reigns of Jeroboam II and Uzziah in the eighth century, once more gaining control of the commercial highways of the region. Jeroboam II reigned in Israel from c. 789 to 748 B.C., and, as we have seen, recovered lands taken earlier by the Syrians, after their power had been broken by the Assyrians. He took control of a large area of Aram. It was under Jeroboam II that the Northern Kingdom of Israel reached its zenith of power: "He . . . restored the borders of Israel from Lebo-Hamath down to the Sea of the Arabah" (2 Kings 14:25).

Peace brought prosperity, luxury, and license. The sanctuaries were thronged with pilgrims, and Israel seemed to be experiencing a religious boom. But the prophets saw only the injustice and immorality of the nation's leaders. Amos, the first great prophet of the eighth century B.C., was a simple shepherd from the south; but God's Word drove him to the Northern Kingdom to denounce Israel's hypocrisy (Amos 5:21–24).

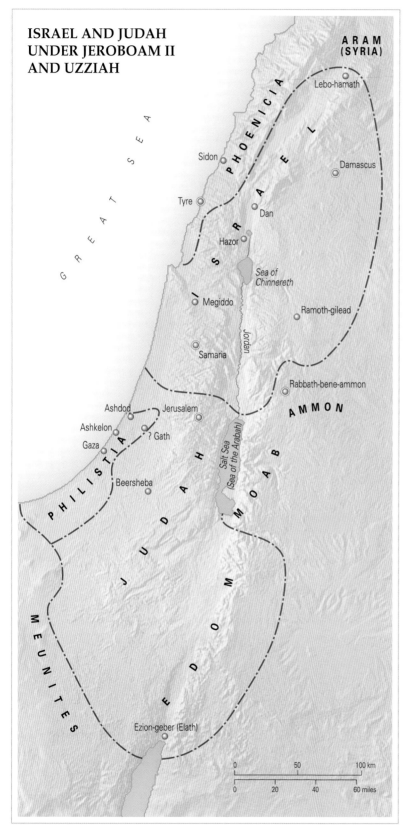

ISRAEL AND JUDAH
UNDER JEROBOAM II
AND UZZIAH

THE SOUTHERN KINGDOM OF JUDAH

The Books of Kings and Chronicles also give an account of the Southern Kingdom, Judah. Its history was not so colorful, and the names of its earlier kings are not so well known, except perhaps for Jehoshaphat, Ahab's contemporary. Judah under Rehoboam was little better than Israel under Jeroboam, for alongside the worship of God the people corrupted themselves with Canaanite fertility rituals. Rehoboam had only been king for four or five years when Shishak of Egypt invaded Jerusalem, plundering the temple of the treasures with which Solomon had enriched it.

King Uzziah reigned in Judah from c. 785 to 734 B.C. He pushed back the frontier with the Philistines and recovered the territory of Edom, which King David had previously conquered. The port of Ezion-geber was rebuilt, giving renewed access to the Red Sea. Uzziah even formed a coalition against Assyria.

The Southern Kingdom continued alone for 136 years more after the fall of the Northern Kingdom. Its period of independence was marked by two religious reforms: the first promoted by King Hezekiah, encouraged by the prophets Isaiah and Micah; the second by King Josiah, encouraged by Zephaniah and Jeremiah.

At the beginning of his reign, Hezekiah repaired and reopened the temple, and removed from his kingdom all traces of the Assyrian idolatry that his father Ahaz had introduced. Meanwhile, Isaiah and Micah denounced idolatry, empty ritual, and social injustice, and called the people to repentance (Micah 6:6–8).

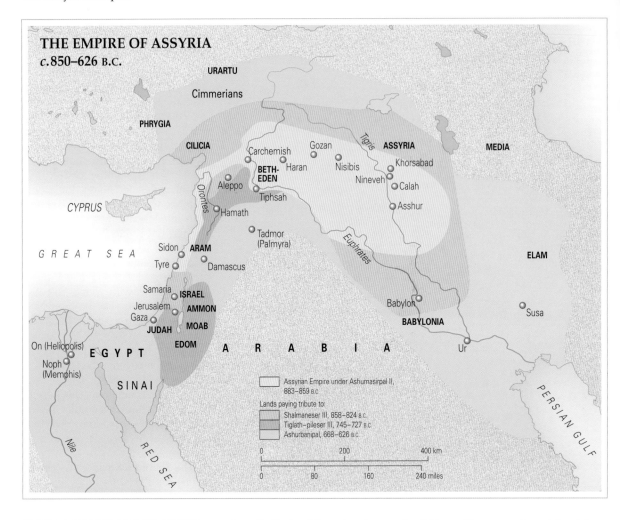

THE EMPIRE OF ASSYRIA
c.850–626 B.C.

URARTU

Cimmerians

PHRYGIA

CILICIA

Carchemish   Gozan   ASSYRIA

Haran   Nisibis   Khorsabad

BETH-
EDEN   Nineveh   Calah

Aleppo

Tiphsah   Asshur

Hamath   Tigris

Tadmor
(Palmyra)   Euphrates

MEDIA

CYPRUS

GREAT SEA

Sidon   ARAM

Tyre   Damascus

Samaria   ISRAEL

Jerusalem   AMMON

Gaza   MOAB

JUDAH   EDOM

ELAM

Babylon   Susa

BABYLONIA

Ur

On (Heliopolis)   EGYPT   A R A B I A

Noph
(Memphis)

SINAI

Nile

RED SEA

PERSIAN GULF

Assyrian Empire under Ashurnasirpal II,
883–859 B.C.

Lands paying tribute to:
Shalmaneser III, 858–824 B.C.
Tiglath–pileser III, 745–727 B.C.
Ashurbanipal, 668–626 B.C.

0		200		400 km
0	80	160	240 miles	

THE ASSYRIAN EMPIRE

Assyria had been a force in Mesopotamia since the fourteenth century B.C. By c. 900 B.C. it was growing into the great empire, which over the next 250 years was feared throughout the ancient Near East. At its maximum extent, the Assyrian Empire stretched from Egypt to the Persian Gulf, though it controlled Egypt only briefly. The capital of the Assyrian Empire shifted: Ashurnasirpal (883–859 B.C.) moved it from Assur to Calah (modern Nimrud); Khorsabad was made capital briefly by Sargon II (721–705 B.C.); and his son Senna-cherib moved it again to Nineveh, where it remained until the fall of the empire.

Israel's first military involvement with Assyria was at the Battle of Qarqar, north of Hamath, when an alliance of twelve kings, including Ahab of Israel, checked the Assyrians' southward advance in 853 B.C. However, Assyria's victory at Damascus in 796 B.C. was a portent of the military prowess she was to demonstrate throughout the following century.

Assyrian relief showing the Israelites bringing tribute to the Assyrians.

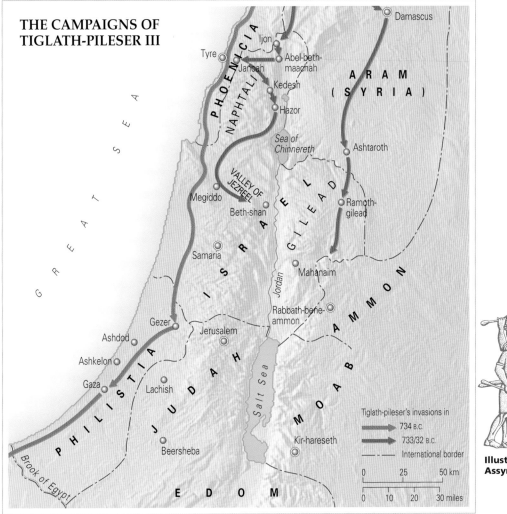

THE CAMPAIGNS OF TIGLATH-PILESER III

Tiglath-pileser's invasions in
→ 734 B.C.
→ 733/32 B.C.
- · - International border

0   25   50 km
0 10 20 30 miles

Illustration of Assyrian spearmen.

THE CAMPAIGNS OF TIGLATH-PILESER III

When the dynasty of Jehu came to an end, the Northern Kingdom had only about thirty years remaining. A succession of military rulers now occupied the throne. But the significant new factor was the rise of the Assyrian Empire. From c. 740 B.C., the Assyrians put Israel and Judah under pressure. Until then the main purpose of Assyrian campaigns in the region had been to secure booty and tribute; already in the middle of the previous century both Ahab and Jehu had paid tribute to King Shalmaneser III. The new king of Assyria, Tiglath-pileser III (745–727 B.C.) ("Pul" in the Bible), now embarked on a series of expansionist campaigns. When Tiglath-pileser reached Israel, he was bought off by King Menahem with 1,000 talents of silver.

A few years later, in 735 B.C., Pekah, who was ruling Israel, made an alliance with Rezin, king of Syria, to throw off the Assyrian yoke. When Ahaz, king of Judah, refused to join them, they invaded his territory. Ahaz now appealed to Tiglath-pileser for help, with devastating results. Tiglath-pileser campaigned down the western flank of the Levant in 734 B.C. One year later, he concentrated on Israel, taking all of Galilee as far south as the Valley of Jezreel. King Pekah was assassinated and his replacement, Hoshea, was obliged to pay a heavy tribute as a vassal king to Assyria (2 Kings 17:3). Syria was overthrown, Galilee and Transjordan were depopulated, and Ahaz paid homage to Tiglath-pileser with silver and gold from the temple.

After Tiglath-pileser's campaigns, the administration of Israel was divided between Assyria and Israel. The northern and eastern parts conquered by Tiglath-pileser were made Assyrian provinces. However, southern Israel was allowed to continue with its own king—at this time Hoshea—provided it remained loyal to Assyria.

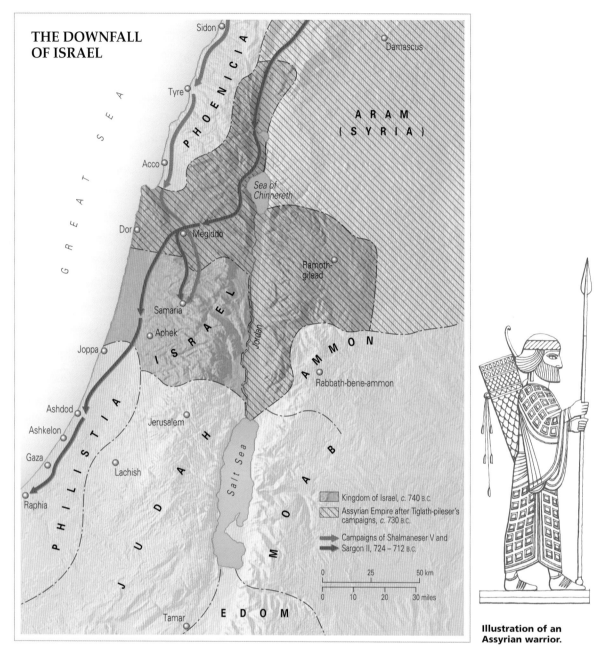

THE DOWNFALL
OF ISRAEL

Sidon
Damascus
Tyre
PHOENICIA
ARAM
(SYRIA)
GREAT SEA
Acco
Sea of
Chinnereth
Dor
Megiddo
Ramoth-
gilead
ISRAEL
Samaria
Aphek
Jordan
AMMON
Joppa
Rabbath-bene-ammon
PHILISTIA
Ashdod
Jerusalem
Ashkelon
JUDAH
Salt Sea
B
Gaza
Lachish
O
Raphia
A
M
Tamar
EDOM

Kingdom of Israel, c. 740 B.C.

Assyrian Empire after Tiglath-pileser's
campaigns, c. 730 B.C.

Campaigns of Shalmaneser V and
Sargon II, 724 – 712 B.C.

0	25	50 km

0	10	20	30 miles

**Illustration of an
Assyrian warrior.**

THE DOWNFALL
OF ISRAEL

When Tiglath-pileser III died,
Samaria withheld its tribute from
Assyria. King Hoshea now also tried
to relieve his people of the heavy
Assyrian tribute by turning to Egypt
for military aid. These reckless acts
provoked the new king of Assyria,
Shalmaneser V, to lay siege to
Samaria. The city capitulated three
years later, probably in 722 B.C., to
his successor Sargon II (2 Kings
17:5–6). Hoshea was arrested and
the inhabitants of Samaria were
deported to different parts of the
Assyrian Empire.

A further campaign under
Sargon II was launched in 720 B.C.
through the western region as far as
Raphia, where the Assyrians were
met by an Egyptian army. The
people of Israel were largely deported, and their country colonized
with Syrians and Babylonians. The
mixed population that resulted was
the origin of the Samaritan people.
In this way the Northern Kingdom
came to an end. It had lasted just
over two centuries.

SENNACHERIB'S CAMPAIGN IN JUDAH

Sargon II, king of Assyria, was killed in battle in 705 B.C., and was succeeded by his son, Sennacherib. King Hezekiah of Judah used the opportunity of the death of Sargon II to rally allies against the mighty Assyria. He was promised support from the Cushites (Ethiopians) and Egyptians, but in the event found only limited help in Philistia. Hezekiah fortified some cities in western Judah and prepared underground water supplies for the eventuality of a siege, with the Siloam tunnel into Jerusalem from the Gihon spring.

In 701 B.C., Sennacherib invaded Phoenicia and many city kings surrendered. Sennacherib continued his campaign south, defeating an Egyptian-Cushite force at El-tekeh. Hezekiah now revolted openly against Assyrian suzerainty. In response, Sennacherib turned inland to the rebel kingdom of Judah and, according to his Assyrian annals, sacked forty-six cities in western Judah, including the heavily fortified city of Lachish. Having taken Judah's fortified cities, Sennacherib next laid siege to Jerusalem itself. As we have seen, Hezekiah had already secured the city's water supply by building a tunnel from the Gihon spring outside the walls to the Pool of Siloam. Even so, the situation seemed desperate.

The Assyrian commander taunted the inhabitants of the beleaguered city (2 Kings 18:19–35), but his siege was suddenly lifted. According to the Bible, "The Angel of the Lord went out and put to death a hundred and eighty-five thousand men in the camp of the Assyrians" (2 Kings 19:35; Isaiah 37:36). Sennacherib did, however, extract a heavy tribute payment from Hezekiah.

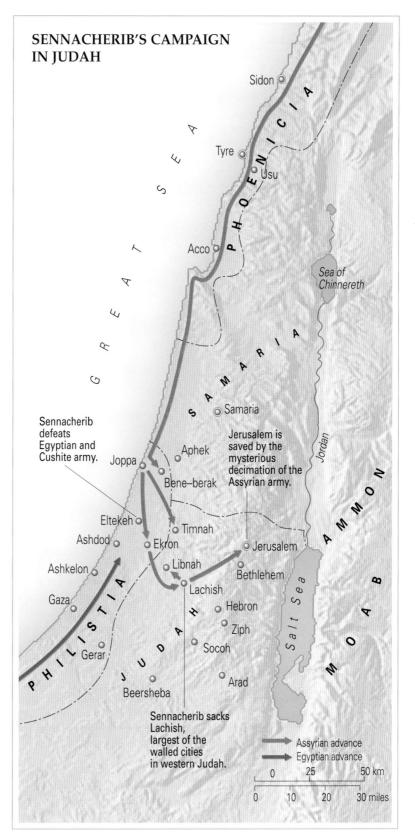

SENNACHERIB'S CAMPAIGN IN JUDAH

Sennacherib defeats Egyptian and Cushite army.

Jerusalem is saved by the mysterious decimation of the Assyrian army.

Sennacherib sacks Lachish, largest of the walled cities in western Judah.

Assyrian advance
Egyptian advance

0   25   50 km
0   10   20   30 miles

53

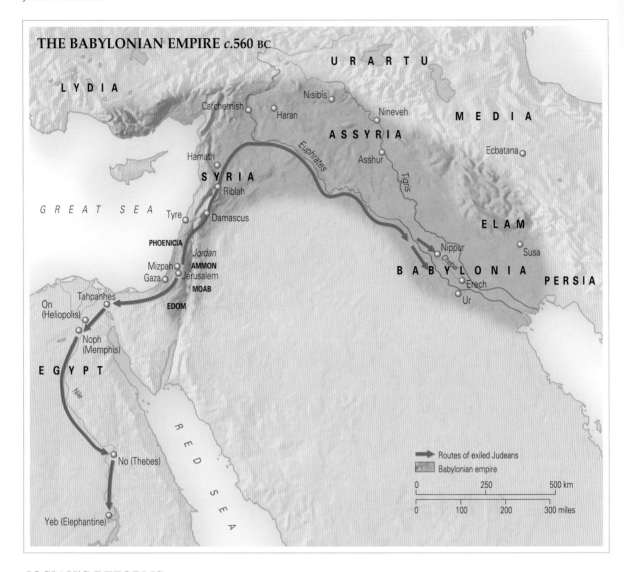

THE BABYLONIAN EMPIRE c.560 BC

URARTU

LYDIA

Carchemish

Nisibis

Haran

Nineveh

MEDIA

ASSYRIA

Ecbatana

Hamath

Asshur

SYRIA

Riblah

GREAT SEA

Tyre

Damascus

ELAM

Euphrates

Tigris

PHOENICIA

Nippur

Susa

Jordan

Chebar

Mizpah

AMMON

BABYLONIA

PERSIA

Gaza

Jerusalem

Erech

MOAB

Ur

On
(Heliopolis)

Tahpanhes

EDOM

Noph
(Memphis)

EGYPT

Nile

No (Thebes)

RED

SEA

Yeb (Elephantine)

Routes of exiled Judeans

Babylonian empire

0   250   500 km

0   100   200   300 miles

JOSIAH'S REFORMS

After Hezekiah's death there followed a period of apostasy. His son Manasseh, a vassal of Assyria, adopted religious syncretism, and reintroduced Canaanite and Assyrian worship, including spiritism, Baal worship, and child sacrifice. Amon, his son, who reigned only two years, was little better.

King Josiah, who reigned from 639 to 609 B.C., turned the scales and introduced more thorough reforms than Hezekiah. He became king of Judah at the age of eight, and as a young man of twenty-six, led the reform of the nation.

During repairs in the temple a book of the law was discovered; this appears to have been part of the Book of Deuteronomy. Josiah summoned the people and read to them from the rediscovered law book. He renewed the nation's covenant with God, had all idolatrous objects removed, closed down local sanctuaries, prohibited spiritism and human sacrifice, and ordered that Passover be celebrated in Jerusalem (2 Kings 23–25).

However, the results of Josiah's reform did not last, and his son Jehoiakim quickly undid the good work. The new king apparently used slave labor to build a palace for himself, and brought upon himself one of the prophet Jeremiah's fieriest denunciations (Jeremiah 22:13–17).

For the previous 200 years Assyria had dominated the Near East, and Israel and Judah had been repeatedly overrun by its armies. But in 616 B.C. Assyria was itself invaded by Nabopolasser, the founder of the Babylonian dynasty, and in 612 B.C. the Assyrian capital, Nineveh, fell after a two-and-a-half-month siege.

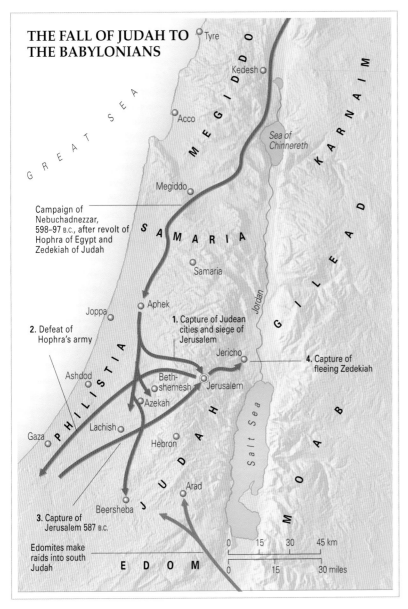

THE FALL OF JUDAH TO THE BABYLONIANS

Tyre

Kedesh

Acco

GREAT SEA

Megiddo

Sea of Chinnereth

Campaign of Nebuchadnezzar, 598–97 B.C., after revolt of Hophra of Egypt and Zedekiah of Judah

SAMARIA

Samaria

Joppa

Aphek

1. Capture of Judean cities and siege of Jerusalem

2. Defeat of Hophra's army

Jericho

4. Capture of fleeing Zedekiah

Ashdod

Beth-shemesh

Jerusalem

Azekah

Salt Sea

Gaza

Lachish

Hebron

PHILISTIA

JUDAH

Arad

Beersheba

3. Capture of Jerusalem 587 B.C.

Edomites make raids into south Judah

EDOM

MEGIDDO

KARNAIM

GILEAD

Jordan

MOAB

0   15   30   45 km

0   15   30 miles

THE FALL OF JUDAH

Even after the fall of Nineveh, Assyria did not immediately concede defeat. In 609 B.C. Pharaoh Neco of Egypt went to her aid, but was defeated by the Babylonians at the Battle of Carchemish in 605 B.C. Now Babylon was supreme, and Judah transferred her homage from Neco to Nebuchadnezzar. Jehoiakim of Judah, who had been put on the throne by the Egyptians, now had to pay tribute to Nebuchadnezzar of Babylon (2 Kings 24:1).

When Nebuchadnezzar's army failed to defeat Neco at the Egyptian border in 601 B.C., Egypt encouraged Judah to rebel against Babylonian control. King Jehoiakim withheld his tribute money; this was tantamount to rebellion. But Jehoiakim died in 598 B.C., before Nebuchadnezzar had time to quell the revolt. However, Jehoiakim did provoke a Babylonian invasion of Judah, in 598 B.C., as well as invasions by Judah's neighboring enemies, in particular the Edomites to the south.

The young Jehoiachin succeeded to the throne of Judah on his father Jehoiakim's death, but was unable to resist the Babylonian pressure. Jerusalem was besieged and captured. Jehoiachin and 3,000 members of the aristocracy were taken captive to Babylon, along with the temple treasures. Among the exiles was Ezekiel, the prophet and priest who had foretold the departure of God's glory from the temple due to Judah's sin.

Nebuchadnezzar appointed Zedekiah, yet another of Josiah's sons, as puppet king of Judah (2 Kings 24:18). He was weak and indecisive. Whereas Zedekiah's counselors advised him to look to Egypt for help, Jeremiah insisted that Judah's only hope lay in submission to Babylon. In 589 B.C. Zedekiah rebelled against Babylon. Hophra of Egypt engaged the Babylonians in the west, but was defeated, and Jerusalem had to endure a second siege in 588 B.C. Jeremiah continued to urge surrender, bringing upon himself first imprisonment and then an attempt on his life.

In spite of holding out for nearly two years, the walls of Jerusalem were finally breached and the city fell. Solomon's magnificent temple was burned to the ground. The inhabitants of Jerusalem were taken into exile in different parts of Babylonia, but many seem to have settled beside the River Chebar (2 Kings 25:1–12).

The tiny remnant of Judah that remained in Jerusalem was put under the charge of Gedaliah, and Jeremiah continued to urge them to submit to Babylon, for this was God's judgment. Gedaliah was assassinated, and the survivors fled to Egypt, dragging Jeremiah with them.

THE RESTORATION FROM BABYLONIAN CAPTIVITY

The Babylonian captivity of Judah lasted about fifty years. Although the exiles had been forcibly deported, they seem to have enjoyed considerable freedom in Babylon. Their hardest trial was religious, for they felt spiritually adrift, separated from the temple and from the sacrifices.

In 559 B.C. Cyrus II ascended the throne of Persia. Nine years later, by defeating the Median army, he also became king of Media, uniting the Medes and Persians. In 546 B.C. Cyrus defeated Croesus, king of Lydia, and added the whole of Asia Minor to his empire.

The Jewish exiles must have heard of the exploits of Cyrus with growing expectation that deliverance from Babylon would come soon. Their prophets always added visions of hope to their warnings of doom (Isaiah 40–55).

In the year 539 B.C. the longed-for salvation came. Belshazzar, king of Babylon, saw the handwriting on the wall, and the same night Babylon fell to the Persians. Immediately, Cyrus issued two decrees, authorizing the Jewish exiles to return home and to rebuild their temple (Ezra 6:3–5). Such edicts are fully consistent with Cyrus's known policy.

However, not all the Jewish exiles took advantage of Cyrus's decree and accepted repatriation; a large number remained in Babylon. Some Jews remained there until modern times. The Book of Esther tells a dramatic story about some of these people during the reign of Ahasuerus (Xerxes I), who ruled the Persian Empire from 486 to 465 B.C.

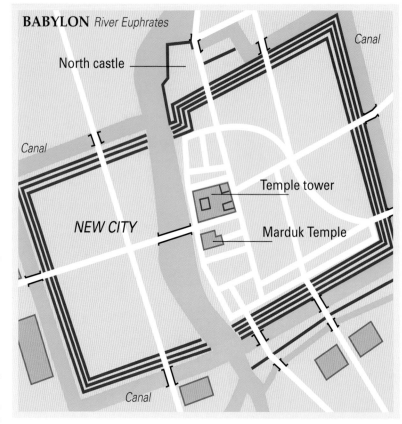

The Cyrus Cylinder recounts how Cyrus captured Babylon and restored the refugees to their native lands.

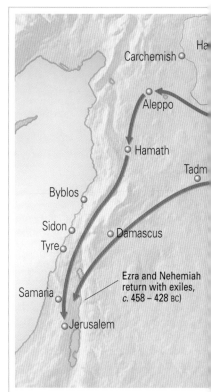

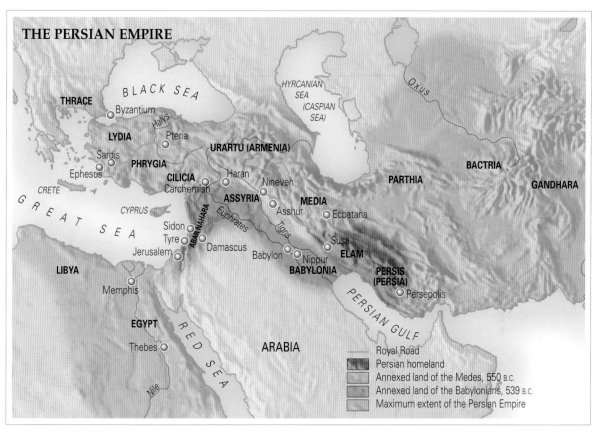

THE PERSIAN EMPIRE

THRACE

BLACK SEA

Byzantium

HYRCANIAN SEA (CASPIAN SEA)

Oxus

Halys

LYDIA

Pteria

URARTU (ARMENIA)

BACTRIA

Sardis

PHRYGIA

Haran

Nineveh

PARTHIA

GANDHARA

Ephesus

CRETE

CILICIA

Carchemish

ASSYRIA

MEDIA

Asshur

Ecbatana

CYPRUS

Euphrates

Tigris

Susa

Sidon

ABAR NAHARA

Damascus

ELAM

GREAT SEA

Tyre

Jerusalem

Babylon

Nippur

BABYLONIA

PERSIS (PERSIA)

LIBYA

PERSIAN GULF

Persepolis

Memphis

EGYPT

RED SEA

ARABIA

Thebes

Nile

Royal Road
Persian homeland
Annexed land of the Medes, 550 B.C.
Annexed land of the Babylonians, 539 B.C.
Maximum extent of the Persian Empire

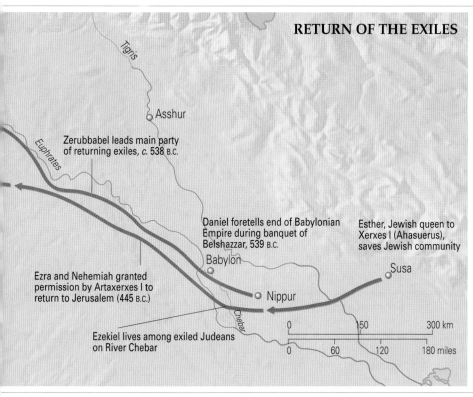

RETURN OF THE EXILES

Tigris

Asshur

Euphrates

Zerubbabel leads main party of returning exiles, *c.* 538 B.C.

Daniel foretells end of Babylonian Empire during banquet of Belshazzar, 539 B.C.

Esther, Jewish queen to Xerxes I (Ahasuerus), saves Jewish community

Babylon

Susa

Ezra and Nehemiah granted permission by Artaxerxes I to return to Jerusalem (445 B.C.)

Nippur

Chebar

Ezekiel lives among exiled Judeans on River Chebar

0		150		300 km
0	60		120	180 miles

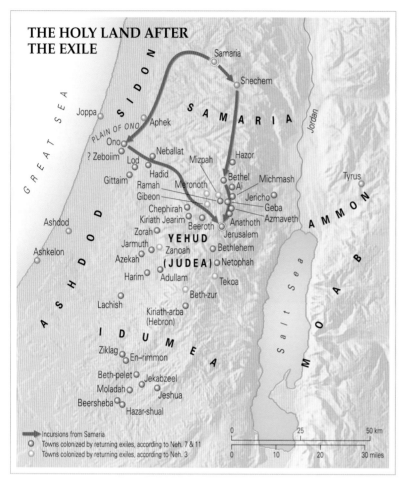

THE HOLY LAND AFTER THE EXILE

Incursions from Samaria
○ Towns colonized by returning exiles, according to Neh. 7 & 11
○ Towns colonized by returning exiles, according to Neh. 3

0   25   50 km
0   10   20   30 miles

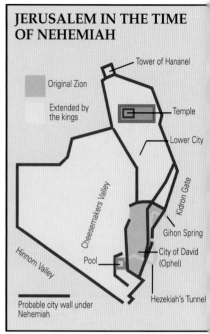

JERUSALEM IN THE TIME OF NEHEMIAH

Original Zion

Extended by the kings

Tower of Hananel
Temple
Lower City
Cheesemakers Valley
Kidron Gate
Gihon Spring
City of David (Ophel)
Hezekiah's Tunnel
Pool
Hinnom Valley

Probable city wall under Nehemiah

EZRA AND NEHEMIAH: THE HOLY LAND AFTER THE EXILE

The restoration of Judah took place in three stages. First, Zerubbabel left (538 B.C.) to restore the temple, then Ezra (458 B.C.) to reinstate the laws, and finally Nehemiah (445 B.C.) to rebuild the city wall.

The first, and main, party of Jews left Babylon for home in 538 B.C., led by Zerubbabel, grandson of King Jehoiachin, and Joshua the high priest. As soon as they arrived in Jerusalem, they built an altar of burnt offering and laid the foundations of the temple. But the initial enthusiasm of the returnees to rebuild Jerusalem was gradually replaced by anxiety about housing

and feeding and about the hostility of neighbors who resented their return. The work of rebuilding the temple halted for about fifteen years.

The work restarted largely due to the encouragement of the prophets Haggai and Zechariah. Haggai reproved the people for building their own houses while the Lord's house still lay ruined (Haggai 2:3–4). Both prophets rebuked the Judeans for being more concerned about their comfort than the restoration of their religious institutions. So the work restarted in 520 B.C. and a revival of interest brought completion of the temple in 516 B.C., about seventy years after the destruction of the previous temple.

Seventy-five years later came the second stage in the reconstruction of Israel's national life, led by Ezra,

a priest and scribe—a kind of "Secretary of State for Jewish Affairs" in Babylonia. He was despatched to Jerusalem by the Persian King Artaxerxes I (465–423 B.C.), with instructions to regulate Israel's religious and moral responsibilities in accordance with the Jewish law (Ezra 7:14).

In 445 B.C., Nehemiah was appointed governor of Judea by Artaxerxes I, with a mandate to complete the rebuilding of Jerusalem's walls (Nehemiah 2:17–18) for greater protection against, among others, Sanballat, governor of Samaria (Nehemiah 4). As we have seen, most of the people of Samaria had been brought there from other lands by the Assyrians after the fall of the Northern Kingdom in 720 B.C. They considered themselves Jews, and the rightful inhabitants of the Holy Land. Mutual resentment between the Jews returning from Babylon and the Samaritans continued into New Testament times.

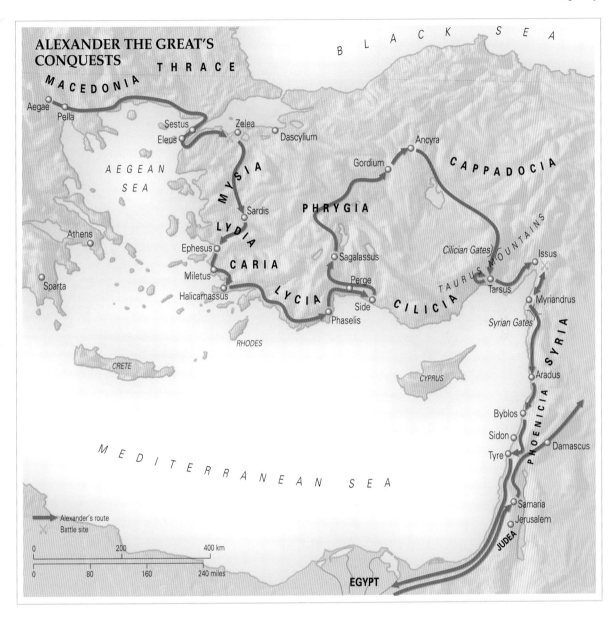

THRACE

MACEDONIA

Aegae

Pella

Sestus

Eleus

Zelea

Dascylium

B L A C K   S E A

Ancyra

CAPPADOCIA

Gordium

AEGEAN SEA

MYSIA

Sardis

PHRYGIA

LYDIA

Cilician Gates

Issus

Athens

Ephesus

CARIA

Sagalassus

TAURUS MOUNTAINS

Miletus

Halicarnassus

LYCIA

Perge

Side

CILICIA

Tarsus

Myriandrus

Sparta

Phaselis

Syrian Gates

SYRIA

RHODES

Aradus

CRETE

CYPRUS

PHOENICIA

Byblos

Sidon

Damascus

Tyre

M E D I T E R R A N E A N   S E A

Samaria

Jerusalem

Alexander's route
Battle site

JUDEA

0   200   400 km

0   80   160   240 miles

EGYPT

Between the Testaments

THE END OF PROPHECY

The classical period of prophecy ended some 400 years before the birth of the Messiah. During that time, some books (Daniel) and portions of books (the latter part of Zechariah) were written as well as a number of books that were written in Greek (e.g., 1 and 2 Maccabees, Wisdom, etc.).

Bust of Alexander the Great based on an extant sculpture.

59

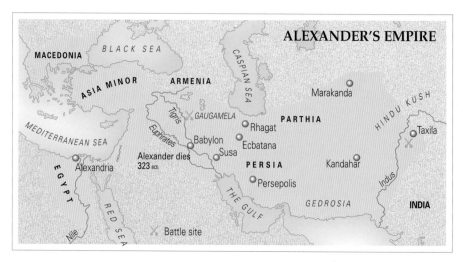

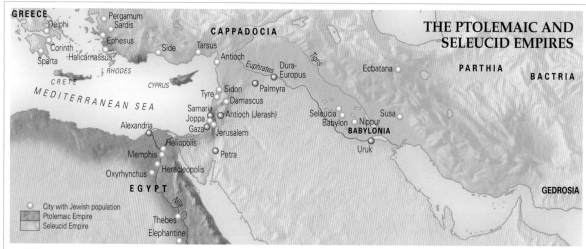

ALEXANDER THE GREAT

Alexander the Great conquered Palestine in 332 B.C. On his death in 323 B.C., his vast and rapidly acquired empire was divided up among his generals. Two opposing empires emerged—the Seleucids of Greece and western Asia, and the Ptolemies of North Africa. Palestine, as a land bridge between the two, became their battleground, and at different times the vassal state of one or the other. In 198 B.C., it became part of the Seleucid Empire.

THE MACCABEAN REVOLT

Pagan worship was instituted in Judea and Samaria as part of the process of hellenization that seeped into Jewish life after the Seleucids came to power. Hellenized Jews from the high priestly families acquiesced in the excesses of the Seleucid ruler, Antiochus IV Epiphanes, who even placed a statue of the Greek god Zeus in the temple and demanded that sacrifices be made to it.

The Maccabean revolt broke out in 167 B.C., when the Jewish high priest Mattathias openly rebelled against the Seleucid authorities, refusing to honor their pagan gods,

and killing a Jewish traitor and the king's officer who was inviting them to sacrifice.

The Maccabee brothers proceeded to lead a series of campaigns against the Seleucid government in a period of guerrilla warfare, during which pagan altars were demolished, Jewish children forcibly circumcised, and compromisers murdered.

Mattathias died in 166 B.C. and was succeeded in turn by three of his sons: Judas, surnamed Maccabaeus, meaning "the hammer" (166–161 B.C.); Jonathan (161–143 B.C.); and Simon (143–135 B.C.). Details of their revolt against Gentile rule and of their military exploits are recorded in 1 and 2

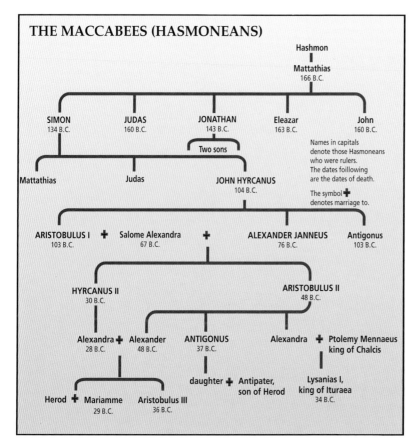

THE MACCABEES (HASMONEANS)

Hashmon

Mattathias
166 B.C.

SIMON	JUDAS	JONATHAN	Eleazar	John
134 B.C.	160 B.C.	143 B.C.	163 B.C.	160 B.C.

Two sons

Names in capitals denote those Hasmoneans who were rulers. The dates foilowing are the dates of death.

The symbol ✚ denotes marriage to.

Mattathias — Judas — JOHN HYRCANUS
104 B.C.

ARISTOBULUS I ✚ Salome Alexandra ✚ ALEXANDER JANNEUS — Antigonus
103 B.C. — 67 B.C. — 76 B.C. — 103 B.C.

HYRCANUS II — ARISTOBULUS II
30 B.C. — 48 B.C.

Alexandra ✚ Alexander — ANTIGONUS — Alexandra ✚ Ptolemy Mennaeus king of Chalcis
28 B.C. — 48 B.C. — 37 B.C.

daughter ✚ Antipater, son of Herod — Lysanias I, king of Ituraea 34 B.C.

Herod ✚ Mariamme — Aristobulus III
29 B.C. — 36 B.C.

until 128 B.C. under John Hyrcanus, Simon's son. Both a priest and leader, John Hyrcanus, helped by his sons, annexed much of the territory surrounding Judea. The kingdom reached its maximum extent under Alexander Jannaeus (103–76 B.C.).

One reason for the success of the Maccabees was the decline in power of the Seleucid Empire. The Parthians were attacking their eastern front, and the Romans were growing increasingly powerful in the west.

The Maccabees, in fact, established a treaty with the Roman Senate that served as the basis for Rome's permission for Jews to be able to practice their religion.

Popularly known as Absalom's Pillar, this tomb in the Kidron Valley outside the old city of Jerusalem possibly dates from the Hasmonean period, and is built in a hellenistic style.

Maccabees. Daniel was also written during this period as a book of encouragement for the persecuted Jews. The Maccabees eventually achieved victory and established a Hasmonean kingdom in the Holy Land in 142 B.C. (1 Maccabees 13:41–42).

Probably the most triumphant moment in their history came in 164 B.C. when, led by Judas Maccabaeus, the temple area was purified and the temple itself restored, a new altar was constructed and dedicated, and the sacrifices began to be offered again. Traditional Jewish ritual was reinstated by descendants of the high-priestly family of Hashmon, who had always been opposed to the hellenizing policy in Judea.

The war of independence continued for many years, and political autonomy was not finally secured

THE HASMONEAN KINGDOM

MEDITERRANEAN SEA

PHOENICIA

Tyre

Antiochia

Gischala

Seleucia

Ptolemais

Sea of Galilee

Gabara

Hippos

Dium

Sepphoris

Geba

Abila

Mount Tabor△

Philoteria

GALILEE

Gadara

Dora

GILEAD

Strato's Tower

Scythopolis

Pella

SAMARIA

Samaria

Gerasa

Mount Gerizim△

Shechem

Apollonia

PEREA

Joppa

Arimathea

Philadelphia

Lydda

JUDEA

Jamnia

Jericho

Emmaus

Samaga

Azotus

Jerusalem

Medeba

Ascalon

Beth-zur

Anthedon

Marisa

Hebron

Gaza

En-gedi

Dead Sea

Orda

Gerar

IDUMEA

MOAB

Raphia

Beersheba

Malatha

Rhinocorura

NABATAEA

Zoar

Independent Judea after Jonathan's campaigns, 142 B.C.
Land conquered by Simon, 142-135 B.C.
John Hyrcanus I, 128-104 B.C.
Aristobulus I, 104-103 B.C.
Alexander Jannaeus, 103-76 B.C.
Boundary of Hasmonean kingdom, 76 B.C.
○ Hellenistic city

| 0 | 25 | 50 km |
| 0 | 10 | 20 | 30 miles |

JEWISH RELIGIOUS PARTIES

Throughout the unstable period of Maccabean rule, important religious movements were growing in the Jewish community, which later hardened into the various parties of Jesus' time.

The revolt of the Maccabees was above all a religious protest, a refusal to compromise with hellenizing. Nothing roused the indignation of the Maccabees more than the time-serving high priests, installed by the Seleucid kings. These are the "renegade Jews" of 1 and 2 Maccabees, who wanted to remove circumcision, copy Greek ways, wear Greek dress, and build a Greek stadium in which to compete.

The Jews who strove to avoid contamination from hellenizing influences were called the **Hasidim**, or pious ones. They were separatists, concerned for religious freedom, and were ancestors of the Pharisees.

The **Hasmoneans** (the Maccabees' family name) wanted not only religious freedom but also national independence. They were involved in political intrigue, and their successors were the Sadducees.

The **Zealots** were political extremists, who wanted to continue the Maccabean struggle for independence. They were revolutionaries, determined to wrest their freedom from Rome, which called them the *Sicarii* or cutthroats, after their favorite form of assassination.

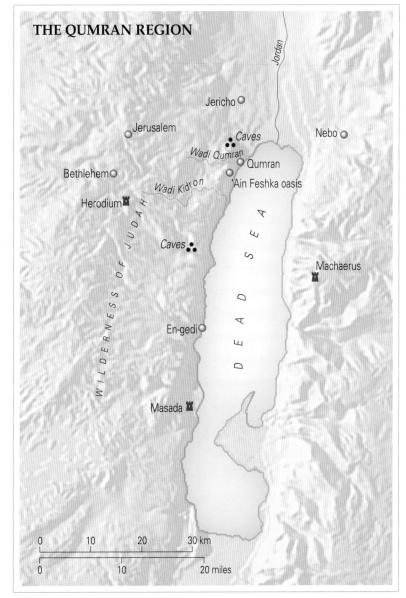

THE QUMRAN REGION

Jordan

Jericho

Jerusalem

Caves

Nebo

Wadi Qumran

Qumran

Bethlehem

'Ain Feshka oasis

Wadi Kidron

Herodium

WILDERNESS OF JUDAH

DEAD SEA

Caves

Machaerus

En-gedi

Masada

| 0 | 10 | 20 | 30 km |

| 0 | 10 | 20 miles |

Orthodox Jewish men pray at Jerusalem's Western Wall, the main remnant surviving from Herod's temple.

63

QUMRAN

The Qumran region, at the north-west end of the Dead Sea, has become famous for the discovery in 1947 of ancient manuscripts, known as the Dead Sea Scrolls. The scrolls contain sections of the Bible and rules of communal discipline. They probably belonged to a monastic community living at Qumran, widely believed to have been the Essenes. The scrolls were found in caves among the hills overlooking Qumran, where they had been hidden from the Romans during the Jewish War of A.D. 66–70.

The settlement at Qumran probably dates from about 145 B.C., after the death of Antiochus Epiphanes IV. The Qumran community may have arisen in opposition to the hellenization of Judaism during his reign. The community practiced strict self-discipline, and interpreted the Old Testament prophecies as referring to current events. They expected the imminent advent of two messiahs, a priestly and a kingly messiah, and considered themselves the remnant of the true Israel, believing that they alone would win God's salvation.

A view of the hills above Qumran from the excavated settlement where a monastic community lived.

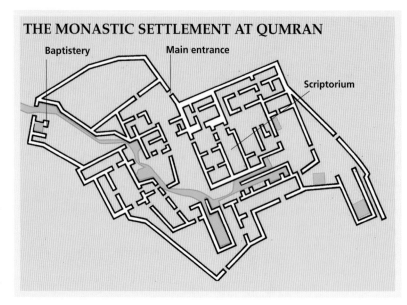

THE MONASTIC SETTLEMENT AT QUMRAN

Baptistery — Main entrance — Scriptorium

Some important Old Testament dates

Year B.C.

c. 1280	The Exodus from Egypt
c. 1050	The monarchy established under King Saul
c. 1010	King David ascends the throne
c. 930	King Solomon dies The divided monarchy begins: Israel lasts until 722, Judah until 586
722	The fall of Samaria and end of the Northern Kingdom
701	Sennacherib besieges Jerusalem
612	The fall of Nineveh, capital of Assyria
597	The fall of Jerusalem The Babylonian captivity begins
586	Jerusalem is destroyed
539	The edict of Cyrus The first exiles return about one year later
516	The restored temple is opened
458	Ezra arrives in Jerusalem
445	Nehemiah arrives in Jerusalem
323	Alexander the Great dies
167	Antiochus Epiphanes profanes the temple The Maccabean revolt begins
63	Pompey reaches Jerusalem: Judea becomes a Roman protectorate

The New Testament

THE FOUR GOSPELS

Although there are a few scattered references to Jesus by contemporary secular writers, such as Tacitus and Suetonius, our main source of information about Jesus is the four Gospels. Their authors selected, arranged, and presented their material according to their purpose.

As we read the Gospels, it becomes clear that they tell the same story, differently. The first three—Matthew, Mark, and Luke—are known as the "Synoptic" Gospels because their stories run parallel and present a similar account of Jesus' life. Matthew and Luke appear to have known Mark's Gospel and incorporated most of it into theirs. They also use some additional common material, generally known as "Q" (the first letter of the German word *Quelle*, source), though each also has independent material. Most scholars believe that John's Gospel was the last to appear.

The Gospel of Mark is the shortest, and probably the earliest, of the four. The style is terse, the stories vivid, and the tone exciting, with everything happening "immediately" after something else. Mark's home in Jerusalem was a meeting place for the first believers (Acts 12:11–12). The Apostle Peter referred to Mark as his son (1 Peter 5:13), and the second-century writers Papias and Irenaeus described him as Peter's interpreter. It

The Holy Family: a sculpture in Nazareth, Jesus' hometown.

may be that Peter's records and memories have been preserved in Mark's Gospel. It is possible that Matthew's name became attached to the first Gospel because "Q," consisting largely of the sayings of Jesus, was his collection. Matthew's Gospel is very Jewish and reveals his interest in the fulfillment of prophecy.

Luke is the only Gentile among all the New Testament authors. He had traveled widely, and, as one of Paul's companions, absorbed the Apostle's teaching about God's grace to the Gentiles. He emphasizes the universal scope of Christ's love, as illustrated in his treatment of the outsiders of contemporary Judaism—women and children, publicans and sinners, lepers, Samaritans, and Gentiles.

John's Gospel is different from the Synoptic Gospels in subject matter, theological emphasis, literary style, and in vocabulary. It is more philosophical in tone, as Jesus is presented as the *Logos* ("Word") of God and the Light of the world. His claims to deity are more outspoken, and the Gospel's framework consists of a series of "signs," interspersed with, and interpreted by, long speeches.

Reliefs over the door to the Basilica of the Annunciation, Nazareth, represent the four Gospel writers, Matthew, Mark, Luke, and John, with their traditional emblems.

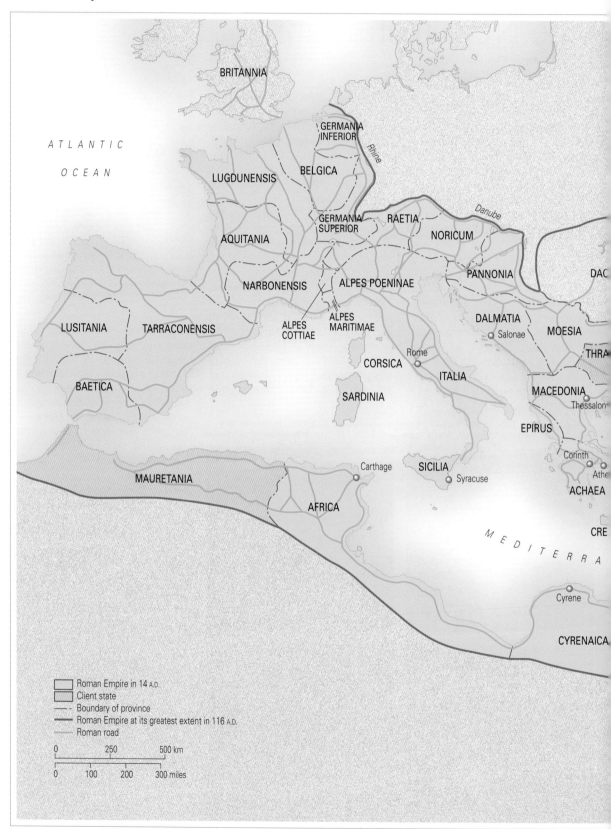

ATLANTIC

OCEAN

BRITANNIA

GERMANIA
INFERIOR

Rhine

BELGICA

LUGDUNENSIS

GERMANIA
SUPERIOR

RAETIA

Danube

NORICUM

AQUITANIA

PANNONIA

DAC

NARBONENSIS

ALPES POENINAE

ALPES
COTTIAE

ALPES
MARITIMAE

DALMATIA

Salonae

MOESIA

LUSITANIA

TARRACONENSIS

THRA

CORSICA

Rome

ITALIA

MACEDONIA

BAETICA

Thessalon

SARDINIA

EPIRUS

Corinth

Athe

ACHAEA

MAURETANIA

Carthage

SICILIA

Syracuse

CRE

AFRICA

M E D I T E R R A

Cyrene

CYRENAICA

	Roman Empire in 14 A.D.
	Client state
–·–	Boundary of province
	Roman Empire at its greatest extent in 116 A.D.
	Roman road

0   250   500 km

0   100   200   300 miles

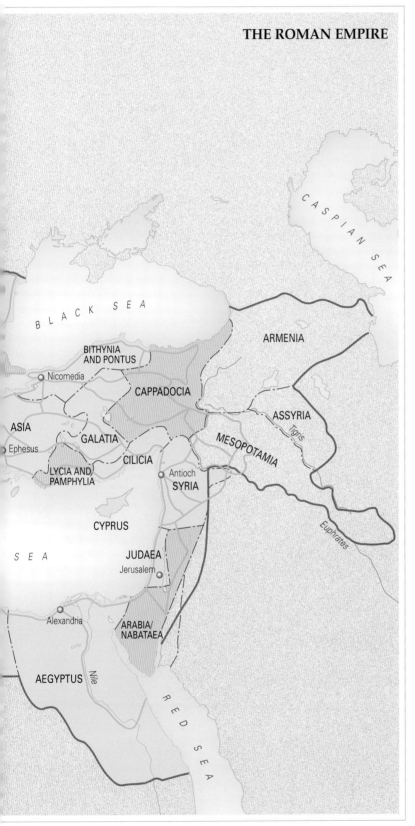

THE ROMAN EMPIRE

CASPIAN SEA

BLACK SEA

ARMENIA

BITHYNIA AND PONTUS

Nicomedia

CAPPADOCIA

ASSYRIA

Tigris

ASIA

GALATIA

MESOPOTAMIA

Ephesus

CILICIA

LYCIA AND PAMPHYLIA

Antioch

SYRIA

CYPRUS

Euphrates

SEA

JUDAEA

Jerusalem

Alexandria

ARABIA/ NABATAEA

AEGYPTUS

Nile

RED SEA

THE ROMAN EMPIRE IN THE TIME OF CHRIST

The Emperor Augustus brought peace, prosperity, and stability to the Roman Empire. By the time of his death in A.D. 14, the frontiers of the empire had been secured: The River Danube became the northern frontier, and a series of buffer states protected the Balkans from Parthia in the east.

Further conquests by the Emperor Trajan (Dacia, Arabia, Armenia, and Mesopotamia) expanded the imperial boundary to its maximum extent in A.D. 116. An extensive program of road-building enabled a Roman citizen to travel safely and quickly; he or she needed no language other than Latin and Greek, no passport, and only the Roman denarius as currency.

The Romans in the Holy Land

In 63 B.C. the Roman general Pompey entered Jerusalem, and penetrated even the holy of holies in the temple, to the horror of the priests. He forced a settlement with the Hasmoneans, by which the Holy Land became a Roman protectorate, and Jewish independence was lost once more.

Sculpted head of the Roman Emperor Augustus, who brought stability to the empire.

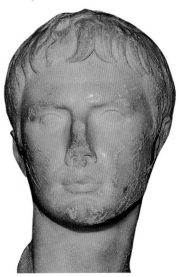

JUDAISM IN THE TIME OF CHRIST

As we have seen, with the coming of the Roman Empire and the *Pax Romana*, the movement of peoples across the Mediterranean world became much easier. Jews were beginning to spread to the west, beyond Italy. They also were able to spread east through the Parthian Empire, and a sizable community had established itself in Babylonia. However, the main areas of concentration remained in Judea, Syria, western Asia Minor, and Egypt, where Alexandria had become a major center of Greek-Jewish culture.

HEROD THE GREAT

In 40 B.C. Herod the Great, who had been military prefect of Galilee and joint tetrarch of Judea, was made "king of the Jews" by the Roman senate. Soon after, the Parthians invaded Syria and the Holy Land and installed their own chosen king, the Hasmonean Mattathias Antigonus. However, Herod gradually reconquered his kingdom, and in 37 B.C. besieged and took Jerusalem, executing Antigonus, the last of the Maccabean priest-rulers. He thus secured the throne for himself and continued to reign until his death in 4 B.C., whereupon the kingdom was divided among his three sons.

Although a Jew by religion, Herod was very unpopular, as he was also an Edomite foreigner. Herod was also very supportive of Roman policy, even erecting shrines to pagan gods. As well as building cities and fortresses outside Jerusalem, Herod the Great made major additions within the city, such as the Temple Mount, the Antonia Fortress, and the Upper Palace. It was also due to Herod that in 19 B.C. the reconstruction of the temple commenced, work that continued almost until A.D. 70, when the temple was again and finally destroyed, this time by the Roman army.

The town of Bethlehem is situated on a hill surrounded today by shepherds' fields and terraced olive groves.

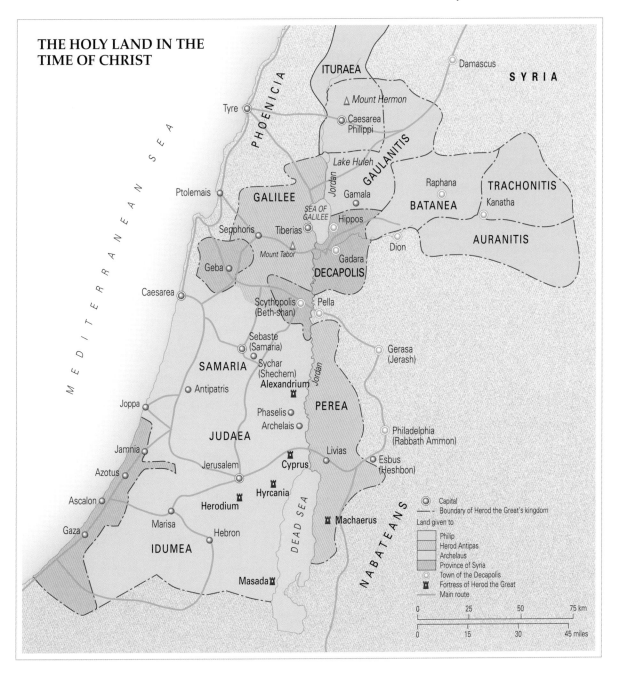

THE HOLY LAND IN THE TIME OF CHRIST

Map labels:

MEDITERRANEAN SEA

ITURAEA
Damascus
SYRIA
Mount Hermon
Caesarea Philippi
PHOENICIA
Tyre
Lake Huleh
Jordan
GAULANITIS
Ptolemais
GALILEE
Gamala
Raphana
TRACHONITIS
Kanatha
BATANEA
SEA OF GALILEE
Sepphoris
Tiberias
Hippos
AURANITIS
Mount Tabor
Dion
Geba
Gadara
DECAPOLIS
Caesarea
Scythopolis (Beth-shan)
Pella
Sebaste (Samaria)
Gerasa (Jerash)
SAMARIA
Sychar (Shechem)
Antipatris
Alexandrium
Jordan
Joppa
Phaselis
PEREA
Archelais
Philadelphia (Rabbath Ammon)
JUDAEA
Jamnia
Livias
Esbus (Heshbon)
Jerusalem
Cyprus
Azotus
Hyrcania
Ascalon
Herodium
NABATEANS
Gaza
Marisa
Hebron
DEAD SEA
Machaerus
IDUMEA
Masada

Legend:

Capital
Boundary of Herod the Great's kingdom
Land given to
Philip
Herod Antipas
Archelaus
Province of Syria
Town of the Decapolis
Fortress of Herod the Great
Main route

0   25   50   75 km
0   15   30   45 miles

THE HOLY LAND IN THE TIME OF CHRIST

Upon the death of Herod, the Holy Land became a province ruled by tetrarchs (literally, ruler of a fourth part, but in practice a provincial ruler more subject to Rome than a king). Archelaus, called Herod the Ethnarch, ruled Judea from 4 B.C. to A.D. 6. He was then sent into exile by the Romans, after complaints about his misgovernment. A Roman governor then ruled Judea until A.D. 41. Herod Antipas ruled Galilee and part of Transjordan from 4 B.C. to A.D. 39; and Herod Philip ruled the northern regions until A.D. 34.

The Decapolis was a confederation of ten cities formed after Pompey's campaign (65–62 B.C.). It gave protection to its Gentile citizens, who were mainly Greek-speaking Roman soldiers, against both militant Jews and Arabian tribes.

THE ECONOMY OF
THE HOLY LAND

Until Roman times Mediterranean trade had been controlled by the Phoenicians. But, with the *Pax Romana*, greater safety allowed more opportunities for commerce, both by sea and over land. The economy was still essentially agrarian: Wheat was grown where possible in the valleys north of Jerusalem, and barley in the south. The hill country provided pasture-land for sheep and cattle, while vines, olives, and dates were the main crops grown on the hillsides.

Metalwork in copper and iron thrived, and by this time there were organized potteries. Jerusalem was a major commercial center, with 118 recorded luxury goods, such as jewelry and silk clothes.

THE BIRTH OF JESUS

Matthew and Luke tell us the story of Jesus' birth, Luke through the eyes of Mary, and Matthew from Joseph's point of view. According to Luke, a Roman census was conducted by Quirinius, governor of Syria, and everyone had to go to their native town to register. Joseph took Mary to his hometown of Bethlehem, where she bore Jesus in the stable of an inn (Luke 2:1–7). There are historic problems with this census for it occurred around 6 A.D., while Jesus was born a number of years earlier.

Although Jesus was born in humble surroundings, some came to pay homage to Him. Luke tells of the Bethlehem shepherds who learned the good news from Angels. Matthew tells of visiting Magi—astrologer-priests from Persia—who followed a star and visited King Herod, asking to see the Child born to be King of the Jews. Herod the Great, who during his reign murdered every possible rival, was naturally anxious about this new contender, and ordered the killing of all babies in

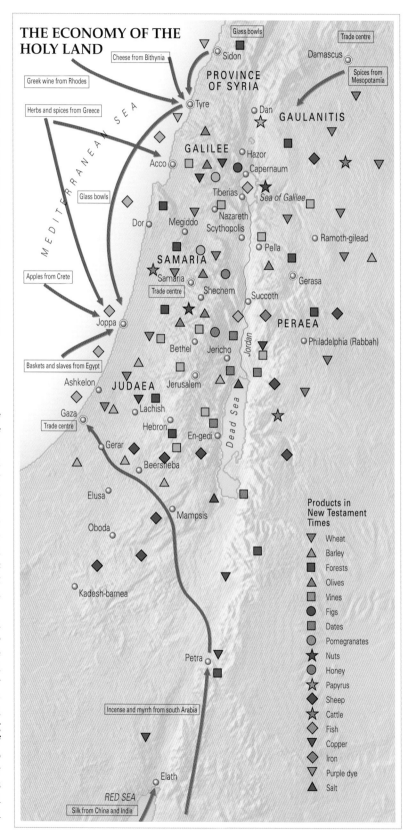

THE ECONOMY OF THE HOLY LAND

Glass bowls
Trade centre
Cheese from Bithynia
Greek wine from Rhodes
Herbs and spices from Greece
Glass bowls
Apples from Crete
Trade centre
Baskets and slaves from Egypt
Trade centre
Spices from Mesopotamia
Incense and myrrh from south Arabia
Silk from China and India

Sidon
Damascus
PROVINCE OF SYRIA
Tyre
Dan
GAULANITIS
GALILEE
Hazor
Acco
Capernaum
Tiberias
Sea of Galilee
Nazareth
Dor
Megiddo
Scythopolis
Pella
Ramoth-gilead
SAMARIA
Samaria
Shechem
Succoth
Gerasa
PERAEA
Joppa
Philadelphia (Rabbah)
Bethel
Jericho
Jordan
Ashkelon
JUDAEA
Jerusalem
Gaza
Lachish
Hebron
En-gedi
Dead Sea
Gerar
Beersheba
Elusa
Mampsis
Oboda
Kadesh-barnea
Petra
Elath
RED SEA
MEDITERRANEAN SEA

Products in New Testament Times
▽ Wheat
△ Barley
■ Forests
△ Olives
▢ Vines
● Figs
▢ Dates
○ Pomegranates
★ Nuts
○ Honey
☆ Papyrus
◆ Sheep
☆ Cattle
◇ Fish
◇ Copper
◇ Iron
▽ Purple dye
▲ Salt

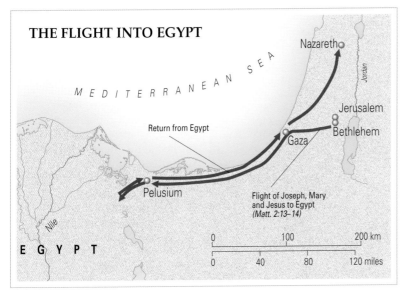

THE FLIGHT INTO EGYPT

Return from Egypt

Flight of Joseph, Mary and Jesus to Egypt (Matt. 2:13–14)

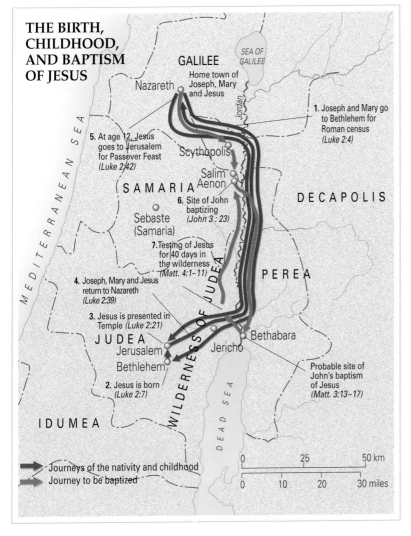

THE BIRTH, CHILDHOOD, AND BAPTISM OF JESUS

GALILEE

Nazareth — Home town of Joseph, Mary and Jesus

1. Joseph and Mary go to Bethlehem for Roman census (Luke 2:4)

5. At age 12, Jesus goes to Jerusalem for Passover Feast (Luke 2:42)

Scythopolis

SAMARIA — Salim Aenon

6. Site of John baptizing (John 3: 23)

DECAPOLIS

Sebaste (Samaria)

7. Testing of Jesus for 40 days in the wilderness (Matt. 4:1–11)

PEREA

4. Joseph, Mary and Jesus return to Nazareth (Luke 2:39)

3. Jesus is presented in Temple (Luke 2:21)

JUDEA — Jerusalem — Bethlehem

Jericho — Bethabara

2. Jesus is born (Luke 2:7)

Probable site of John's baptism of Jesus (Matt. 3:13–17)

IDUMEA

DEAD SEA

Journeys of the nativity and childhood
Journey to be baptized

and around Bethlehem. Joseph and Mary fled to Egypt to escape the slaughter (Matthew 2:1–18).

THE CHILDHOOD OF JESUS

After Herod's death Mary and Joseph went to Nazareth, which was under the rule of Herod Antipas, for it was too dangerous to return to Bethlehem, which was ruled by the tyrant Archelaus. Jesus was brought up in this unimportant little town in Galilee, where Joseph worked as a carpenter and probably taught his trade to the young Boy.

The only incident from Jesus' boyhood recorded in the Gospels took place when he reached the age of twelve and was taken to Jerusalem for the Passover, following Jewish tradition, to prepare to become a "son of the commandment." After setting off on the return trip, Jesus' parents discovered that He was not with them—presumably they were in a crowd and had not noticed. They went back to Jerusalem and found Him debating with the elders. These Jewish leaders were amazed at His understanding; while His parents were puzzled when He asked: "Did you not know that I must be in My Father's house?" (Luke 2:41–51).

Finally they headed back to Nazareth. Jews traveling between Nazareth and Jerusalem would normally cross to the far side of the River Jordan, to avoid Samaria. What would be a three-day journey on foot via Samaria was made twice as long by going through Transjordan.

Model of Herod's temple. Jesus' parents found Him in the temple court, debating with the Jewish rabbis.

THE FIRST YEAR OF JESUS' MINISTRY

John the Baptist was an ascetic, who wore only a camel's hair cloak, and ate locusts and wild honey. He summoned people to repent and to be baptized in preparation for the coming of the Messiah. Crowds flocked to the River Jordan to listen to him.

When Jesus presented Himself for Baptism, John protested, saying that he was unworthy to undo the sandal of the One coming after him. But Jesus persuaded John to baptize Him. At that moment the Holy Spirit came upon Jesus, and the Father's voice proclaimed Him to be His beloved Son. Immediately after His Baptism, the Spirit drove Jesus into the Judean desert, where He fasted for forty days. After this period He was tempted by the devil.

After the temptation, Jesus called the brothers Andrew and Simon Peter to serve Him. They left John the Baptist and began to follow Jesus. Returning to Galilee, Jesus performed His first miracle, chang-

Left: Nazareth and the Basilica of the Annunciation from the hill overlooking the town. The "Mount of Precipitation" is in the background.

Below: The traditional Baptismal site on the River Jordan, at the southern end of Lake Tiberias (Sea of Galilee).

JESUS' MINISTRY IN GALILEE

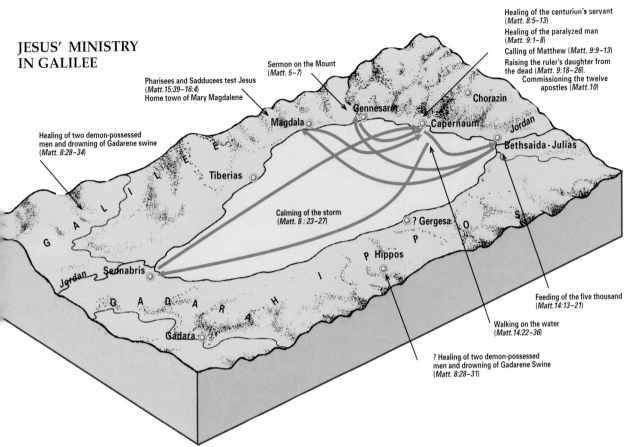

Healing of the centurion's servant (*Matt. 8:5–13*)

Healing of the paralyzed man (*Matt. 9:1–8*)

Calling of Matthew (*Matt. 9:9–13*)

Raising the ruler's daughter from the dead (*Matt. 9:18–26*).

Commissioning the twelve apostles (*Matt. 10*)

Sermon on the Mount (*Matt. 5–7*)

Pharisees and Sadducees test Jesus (*Matt. 15:39–16:4*)
Home town of Mary Magdalene

Healing of two demon-possessed men and drowning of Gadarene swine (*Matt. 8:28–34*)

Calming of the storm (*Matt. 8:23–27*)

Feeding of the five thousand (*Matt. 14:13–21*)

Walking on the water (*Matt. 14:22–36*)

? Healing of two demon-possessed men and drowning of Gadarene Swine (*Matt. 8:28–31*)

Chorazin, Capernaum, Jordan, Bethsaida - Julias, Gennesaret, Magdala, Tiberias, ? Gergesa, Hippos, Sennabris, Jordan, Gadara, GALILEE, GADARA, HIPPOS

---

ing water into wine at a wedding in Cana (John 2:1–11). Then he went to Jerusalem for Passover, ejecting from the temple traders and money-changers who were polluting it.

Jesus visited Jerusalem several times during His ministry, mainly to celebrate the great festivals (John 2:13; 5:1; 7:10; 10:22–23). He stayed in Bethany at the house of Lazarus and his sisters, Mary and Martha (John 11).

One man impressed by Jesus was the Pharisee, Nicodemus. Jesus told him that the condition for entering God's kingdom was new birth by the power of the Holy Spirit (John 3). Later, on His way north to Galilee, Jesus repeated this message to a Samaritan woman (John 4).

No other details of the first year of Jesus' ministry are recorded, though most of it seems to have been spent in Judea. In this period, Jesus' ministry overlapped with that of John the Baptist. Gradually those following Jesus began to outnumber those following John, something that John accepted, saying: "He must increase; I must decrease" (John 3:30).

Jesus then left Judea for Galilee. Soon afterward John was arrested and imprisoned, and Jesus' Galilean ministry began (John 3:24; 4:1–3; Mark 1:14).

JESUS' MINISTRY IN GALILEE

Galilee was a much more prosperous region than Judea, and supported a large population. The Galileans were despised by the religious leaders in Jerusalem. Many were not Jews by descent, their forebears having been forcibly converted by Alexander Jannaeus. However, the Galileans were probably more closely in touch with the daily reality of the Roman Empire, as Galilee lay on the great trade routes that crossed the Near East, and many foreigners passed through the region.

Attending synagogue one sabbath in His hometown of Nazareth, Jesus read aloud from the Isaiah scroll: "The Spirit of the Lord is upon Me, because He has anointed Me to bring the good news to the poor. He has sent Me to proclaim release to prisoners and recovery of sight to the blind, to let the oppressed go free . . ." (Luke 4:18).

Jesus went on to claim that He fulfilled this Scripture. When He suggested that His ministry would be more acceptable to Gentiles than to Israel, the people were so outraged that they drove Him out of the city and tried to push Him off a nearby hill. He now had to move from Nazareth to Capernaum, on the northwest shore of the lake.

SEA OF GALILEE

Archaeological excavations have revealed that there were in all twelve towns on the shores of the lake. The preservation of fish by salting and its export across the Roman Empire was a major industry. The city of Tiberias, built by Antipas (c. A.D. 18) to commemorate the Roman emperor, was one of the main fishing centers.

Much of Jesus' ministry took place around the Sea of Galilee. He often taught in a boat while the crowds listened from the shore. Crossings were frequently made to the other side, and Jesus' earliest Apostles were local fishermen (Mark 1:14–20). The lake was large and subject to sudden squalls as winds swept across the valley: hence the unexpected storm at sea (Mark 4:35–41).

The location of the drowning of the Gadarene swine is disputed (Mark 5:1–20). It may have been at the foot of the hill near the inland village of Gadara, at the southern end of the Sea of Galilee; or it may have been the traditional site at Kursi (perhaps Gergesa) on the eastern shore.

From Capernaum, during His second year's ministry, Jesus journeyed throughout Galilee, "teaching in their synagogues, proclaiming the good news of the kingdom, and curing every type of disease and illness" (Matthew 4:23; 9:35).

Jesus also taught His disciples the law of the kingdom, summarized in the Sermon on the Mount. He called His disciples to be different from pagans and Pharisees; if they were to be the light of the world and the salt of the earth, their righteousness had to be greater than that of the scribes and Pharisees. His disciples must be different from the Gentiles too; they must love their enemies as well as their friends, avoid vain repetitions in prayer,

Sea of Galilee (Tiberias) from the traditional site of the Mount of the Beatitudes.

Part of the reconstructed third-century synagogue at Capernaum.

and seek not their own material needs but the righteousness of God.

Jesus reinforced His teaching with memorable parables, illustrating the love of God for sinners, the need for trust in God's mercy, the love we should have for one another, the way God's Word comes and God's kingdom grows, the responsibility of disciples to develop their gifts,

and the judgment on those who reject the Gospel.

Jesus' most common miracles were healing miracles, effected by a touch or by a command. His miracles were "signs" of God's kingdom, showing that the Messiah's reign had begun, as the Scriptures had foretold. Jesus also performed miracles that demonstrated His power over nature: by stilling a

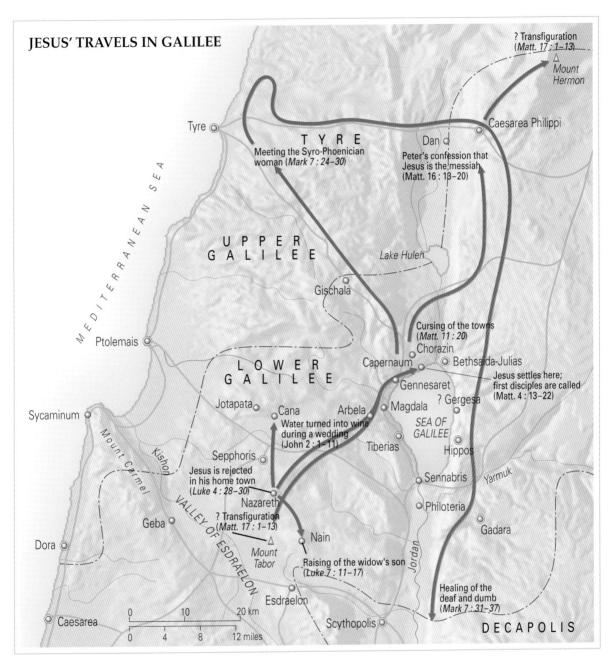

JESUS' TRAVELS IN GALILEE

? Transfiguration
(*Matt. 17 : 1–13*)

Mount Hermon

Tyre

T Y R E

Dan

Caesarea Philippi

Meeting the Syro-Phoenician
woman (*Mark 7 : 24–30*)

Peter's confession that
Jesus is the messiah
(Matt. 16 : 13–20)

MEDITERRANEAN SEA

U P P E R
G A L I L E E

Lake Huleh

Gischala

Ptolemais

Cursing of the towns
(*Matt. 11 : 20*)

Chorazin

L O W E R
G A L I L E E

Capernaum

Bethsaida-Julias

Jesus settles here;
first disciples are called
(Matt. 4 : 13–22)

Gennesaret

? Gergesa

Jotapata

Cana

Arbela

Magdala

Sycaminum

Water turned into wine
during a wedding
(John 2 : 1–11)

SEA OF
GALILEE

Tiberias

Hippos

Sepphoris

Jesus is rejected
in his home town
(Luke 4 : 28–30)

Sennabris

Yarmuk

Nazareth

Mount Carmel

Kishon

Geba

? Transfiguration
(*Matt. 17 : 1–13*)

Philoteria

Dora

Mount
Tabor

Nain

Gadara

VALLEY OF ESDRAELON

Jordan

Raising of the widow's son
(*Luke 7 : 11–17*)

Esdraelon

0   10   20 km

0   4   8   12 miles

Caesarea

Scythopolis

Healing of the
deaf and dumb
(*Mark 7 : 31–37*)

D E C A P O L I S

storm on the lake, by walking on water, and by multiplying the loaves and fish.

Jesus involved the Twelve in His preaching, teaching, and healing ministry. He seems to have called them early in the second year of His ministry and, by naming them "Apostles," indicated their task. They were an unpromising group, including four fishermen, one tax-collector, at least one political Zealot, and another who was to become a traitor. Yet Jesus trained them, and sent them out two by two, giving them His authority to preach and heal.

During the Galilean ministry the crowds kept growing. The whole region became excited and expectant (Luke 5:15). The peak of Jesus' popularity seems to have been reached at the time of the feeding of the 5,000, just after the beheading of John the Baptist. After the hunger of all had been satisfied, word began to go around, "This is indeed the Prophet Who is to come." They determined to make Him king by force—their national leader to liberate them from the dominion of Rome. But Jesus withdrew to the hills by Himself (John 6:14–15).

75

JESUS' MINISTRY: THE FINAL YEAR

Having returned to Capernaum, Jesus preached a sermon in the synagogue, explaining that He had come not as a political revolutionary, but as the Bread of Life. The bread He would give was His flesh. The Jews were offended: "How can this Man give us His flesh to eat?" Even His disciples found it a hard saying, and many now stopped following Him (John 6:52, 66).

Jesus withdrew again, journeying beyond Galilee. He went to Tyre and Sidon in the northwest (Mark 7:24), and to the Decapolis, southeast of the lake (Mark 7:31). Later He traveled north again, this time to Caesarea Philippi, in the foothills of Mount Hermon (Mark 8:27). Here Jesus asked the Twelve who people were saying He was. They told Him John the Baptist, Elijah, or one of the prophets. When He asked who the Twelve thought He was, Peter replied: "You are the Christ." Jesus ordered them to tell no one (Mark 8:29–30), and began to teach that He must suffer, be killed, and after three days rise again (Mark 8:31–32).

Six days later, Jesus took Peter, James, and John with Him up a high mountain (possibly Mount Tabor) and was transfigured, His face and clothing shining with light.

When Jesus returned to Galilee, it was largely a private visit; He continued to teach the disciples about His coming sufferings and Resurrection (Mark 9:30–31). Soon after, He began to travel south (Mark 10:1), aiming for Jerusalem (Luke 9:51), and en route continued to teach them (Mark 10:32–34, 45; Luke 9:51–18:14).

They approached Jerusalem via Jericho, an ancient oasis near where the Jordan flows into the Dead Sea. Here Jesus brought sight to blind Bartimaeus and salvation to Zacchaeus the crooked tax-collector (Luke 18:35–19:10). Then they made

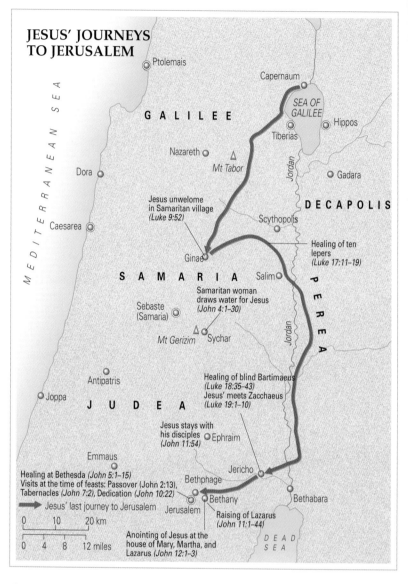

JESUS' JOURNEYS TO JERUSALEM

Ptolemais
Capernaum
SEA OF GALILEE
GALILEE
Hippos
Tiberias
Nazareth
Mt Tabor
Gadara
Dora
DECAPOLIS
Jesus unwelome in Samaritan village (Luke 9:52)
Scythopolis
Caesarea
Healing of ten lepers (Luke 17:11–19)
Ginae
SAMARIA
Salim
P E R E A
Samaritan woman draws water for Jesus (John 4:1–30)
Sebaste (Samaria)
Mt Gerizim
Sychar
Jordan
Antipatris
Healing of blind Bartimaeus (Luke 18:35–43)
Joppa
Jesus' meets Zacchaeus (Luke 19:1–10)
J U D E A
Jesus stays with his disciples (John 11:54)
Ephraim
Emmaus
Jericho
Healing at Bethesda (John 5:1–15)
Visits at the time of feasts: Passover (John 2:13), Tabernacles (John 7:2), Dedication (John 10:22)
Bethphage
Bethany
Bethabara
Jesus' last journey to Jerusalem
Jerusalem
Raising of Lazarus (John 11:1–44)
0   10   20 km
0   4   8   12 miles
Anointing of Jesus at the house of Mary, Martha, and Lazarus (John 12:1–3)
DEAD SEA

the steep climb toward the holy city. John's Gospel records that Jesus spent about six months in Judea, including visits to Jerusalem for the Feast of Tabernacles in October and the Feast of Dedication in December (John 7:2, 10, 14; 10:22–23).

When Jesus appeared for the festivals, His claims became bolder. He declared that He was the Giver of living water, the Light of the world, the great "I am," the Good Shepherd, and the Resurrection and the Life (John 7:37–39; 8:12; 9:5; 8:58; 10:11; 11:25–26). Jewish leaders found these claims provocative, and

several times tried to arrest and kill Him (John 5:18; 7:30, 32; 8:59; 10:39; 11:53, 57).

Already during His Galilean ministry, although the crowds supported Him loudly, Jesus had attracted criticism from the scribes and Pharisees. He was accused of blasphemy, consorting with sinners, religious laxity, and sabbath-breaking (Mark 2:1–28). Defending Himself, Jesus had made matters worse in His critics' eyes by claiming to be the Son of Man.

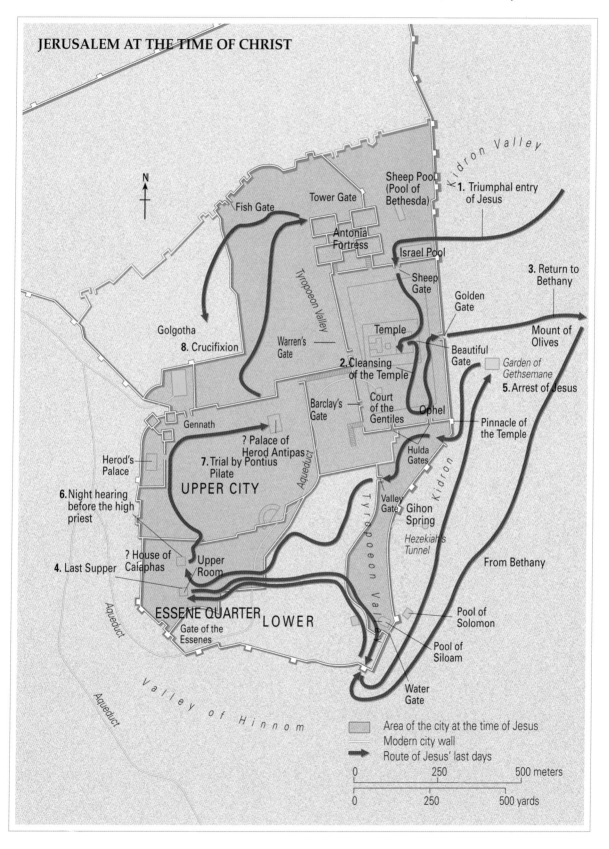

JERUSALEM AT THE TIME OF CHRIST

N

Kidron Valley

Sheep Pool (Pool of Bethesda)

1. Triumphal entry of Jesus

Tower Gate

Fish Gate

Antonia Fortress

Israel Pool

Sheep Gate

3. Return to Bethany

Golden Gate

Temple

Tyropoeon Valley

Warren's Gate

Golgotha

8. Crucifixion

Beautiful Gate

Mount of Olives

2. Cleansing of the Temple

Garden of Gethsemane

5. Arrest of Jesus

Court of the Gentiles

Ophel

Barclay's Gate

Pinnacle of the Temple

Gennath

? Palace of Herod Antipas

Hulda Gates

Herod's Palace

7. Trial by Pontius Pilate

UPPER CITY

Aqueduct

Valley Gate

Kidron

6. Night hearing before the high priest

Gihon Spring

Hezekiah's Tunnel

Tyropoeon Valley

From Bethany

? House of Caiaphas

Upper Room

4. Last Supper

ESSENE QUARTER

LOWER

Pool of Solomon

Gate of the Essenes

Pool of Siloam

Aqueduct

Valley of Hinnom

Water Gate

Aqueduct

Area of the city at the time of Jesus

Modern city wall

Route of Jesus' last days

| 0 | 250 | 500 meters |
| 0 | 250 | 500 yards |

The Temple Mount, Jerusalem, viewed from the slopes of the Mount of Olives.

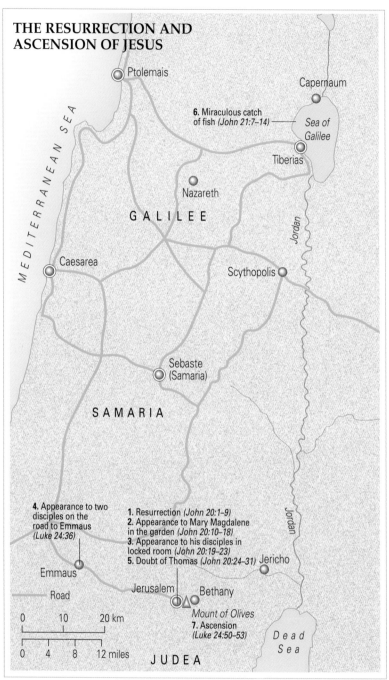

THE RESURRECTION AND ASCENSION OF JESUS

Ptolemais

Capernaum

6. Miraculous catch
of fish *(John 21:7–14)* — *Sea of
Galilee*

Tiberias

Nazareth

GALILEE

Jordan

Caesarea

Scythopolis

Sebaste
(Samaria)

SAMARIA

4. Appearance to two
disciples on the
road to Emmaus
(Luke 24:36)

1. Resurrection *(John 20:1–9)*
2. Appearance to Mary Magdalene
in the garden *(John 20:10–18)*
3. Appearance to his disciples in
locked room *(John 20:19–23)*
5. Doubt of Thomas *(John 20:24–31)*

Jordan

Jericho

Emmaus

Jerusalem   Bethany

Road

Mount of Olives
7. Ascension
(Luke 24:50–53)

*Dead
Sea*

0   10   20 km

0   4   8   12 miles

JUDEA

Jesus condemned the Pharisees who opposed Him for their hypocrisy (see, for example, Luke 11:37–52) and their man-made traditions (Mark 7:1–13), and the Sadducees for their ignorance of God's Word and power (Mark 12:18–27). The tensions grew. The Jewish leaders were jealous of His popularity, wounded by His exposure of them, and shamed by His integrity. It was only a matter of time before the showdown.

Approaching Jerusalem for the last time, Jesus reached the point on the Mount of Olives where the city came into view, and then wept (Luke 19:41–44). He had arranged to ride into Jerusalem on a borrowed donkey, to fulfill the prophecy of Zechariah (Zechariah 9:9; Matthew 21:5). The crowds were eager to greet Him, waving palm branches in the air and shouting "Hosanna." But His triumph was not shared by the authorities. Jesus antagonized them further by cleansing the temple again (Mark 11:15–18), and during the next three days, from Monday to Wednesday, their hostility became increasingly focused.

JESUS' DEATH AND RESURRECTION

The Thursday of Jesus' last week is believed to have been either Passover eve or Passover itself. Jesus spent His final hours of freedom with the Twelve in a borrowed Upper Room. Here, they ate the Passover meal together. During supper, Jesus washed the feet of the Twelve, a slave's work, and gave them bread and wine as His Body and Blood. He told them to eat and drink in His memory.

It is believed that Stephen was martyred outside this gate into the city of Jerusalem.

Late in the evening they left the room, walked through the city, crossed the Kidron Valley, and began to climb the Mount of Olives, arriving at the Garden of Gethsemane. Soon temple soldiers arrived to arrest Jesus, and Judas betrayed Him to them.

That night and the next morning Jesus faced a number of separate trials: in Jewish courts; before Herod; and before Pontius Pilate, known to have the blood of many Jews on his hands (Luke 13:1). Herod's palace was the residence of the Roman governors. It was most likely that Jesus was tried here by Pontius Pilate (Matthew 27:11–26). It is also possible that He was tried at Herod Antipas's palace.

When false witnesses accused Him, Jesus was silent. But when the high priest asked if He was the Christ, the Son of God, Jesus acknowledged that He was, and was instantly condemned to death for blasphemy. Since by Roman law the Jews were not allowed to carry out the death sentence, they needed to have it ratified by the procurator. Pilate quickly saw through the political charge brought against Jesus, and was soon satisfied that

the prisoner was no revolutionary. But Pilate was concerned when the Jewish leaders hinted that, if Pilate released Jesus, he would forfeit Caesar's favor, and handed Jesus over to them to be flogged and crucified.

Jesus was crucified in a used-out rock quarry that was then being used as a garbage dump. A mound of rock shaped something like a skull (hence the name Golgotha, the place of the skull) had been left there because it was filled with cracks. One of these cracks probably served as the foundation of the Cross.

Joseph of Arimathea and Nicodemus buried Jesus in a tomb that lay nearby. Pilate ordered guards to be placed at the tomb's entrance to prevent Jesus' disciples from "stealing" the body.

At first light on Easter day, Mary Magdalene and some other women came to the tomb, to complete the burial rites for Jesus, which the coming of the sabbath had interrupted. But they found the stone rolled away from the entrance to the tomb and the tomb empty.

The risen Lord now began to appear to people: first to Mary Magdalene and to Peter; then to two disciples on the road from Jerusalem to Emmaus; then to the Apostles that same evening; again when Thomas (previously absent) was with them; next, when they returned to Galilee—on a mountain and beside the lake. On this last occasion He commissioned them to go into the whole world and to make all nations His disciples.

These appearances continued for forty days. The final appearance took place on the Mount of Olives. Having promised the disciples power to be His witnesses when the Holy Spirit had come on them, He was taken up into heaven. So they returned rejoicing to Jerusalem to await the coming of the Holy Spirit in power, as Jesus had promised.

THE INFANT CHURCH

Suddenly, while the disciples were praying together, the Holy Spirit came and filled them. Foreigners in the crowd were able to understand the disciples, although they were speaking in Aramaic. Three thousand people were converted, baptized, and added to the Church that day. The believers devoted themselves to the Apostles' teaching, to fellowship, to breaking of bread, and to prayer (Acts 2:42).

But even in the infant Church there were problems. When Peter and John started to proclaim Jesus (Acts 4:1–2), they were arrested and tried before the Jewish court, the Sanhedrin. After being threatened, they were released. The Apostles went back to their Christian friends and prayed for courage to continue preaching. They were again arrested, and now imprisoned; but an Angel released them and told them to preach the Gospel in the temple precincts. Once more Peter and John were arrested and tried, this time by the Jewish Council. After the Pharisee Gamaliel warned that the Council might be opposing God, they only beat them and ordered them again not to speak in Jesus' name. Day after day, in the temple courts and from house to house, they proclaimed the Gospel continually (Acts 5:41–42).

The Word of God spread, and the number of disciples in Jerusalem increased rapidly (Acts 6:7). The Apostles instructed the believers to choose seven deacons to take over the welfare work, so that they could devote themselves to prayer and preaching. One of the seven deacons, Stephen, was accused of speaking against the law of Moses and the temple. He was brought before the Jewish Council who threw him out of the city and stoned him to death. After Stephen's martyrdom on the charge of blasphemy (Acts 6:11), many of the Apostles left Jerusalem and began to preach the Gospel elsewhere.

CHRISTIANITY IN THE HOLY LAND BEFORE PAUL

The persecution of Christians scattered them throughout Judea and Samaria (Acts 8:1). Philip, Peter, and John all made conversions in Samaria (Acts 8), a "no-go" area for religious (or "strict") Jews. Philip, another of the seven deacons, also explained the Gospel to an Ethiopian official on his way home from Jerusalem (Acts 8:26–39). The coastal plain of Judea, as far north as Caesarea, was also evangelized by Peter and Philip. As the persecution of Christians by Jews in Jerusalem became more persistent, so Jewish Christians dispersed northward.

This outreach was the prelude to the Gentile mission, which began with the conversion of Saul of Tarsus and, through Peter, the conversion of the Roman centurion, Cornelius. Paul and Peter were crucial in opening the Church to Gentiles.

Below: Remains of the great Roman harbor at Caesarea Maritima, on the Mediterranean coast of the Holy Land, can be seen at low tide.

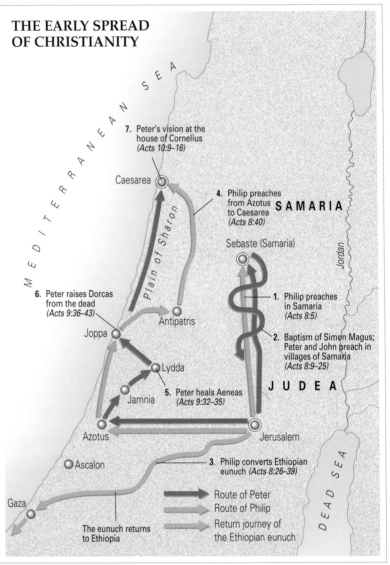

THE EARLY SPREAD OF CHRISTIANITY

7. Peter's vision at the house of Cornelius (*Acts 10:9–16*)

4. Philip preaches from Azotus to Caesarea (*Acts 8:40*)

Caesarea

S A M A R I A

Sebaste (Samaria)

1. Philip preaches in Samaria (*Acts 8:5*)

6. Peter raises Dorcas from the dead (*Acts 9:36–43*)

Antipatris

Joppa

2. Baptism of Simon Magus; Peter and John preach in villages of Samaria (*Acts 8:9–25*)

Lydda

Jamnia

5. Peter heals Aeneas (*Acts 9:32–35*)

J U D E A

Azotus

Jerusalem

Ascalon

3. Philip converts Ethiopian eunuch (*Acts 8:26–39*)

Gaza

The eunuch returns to Ethiopia

MEDITERRANEAN SEA

Plain of Sharon

Jordan

DEAD SEA

→ Route of Peter
→ Route of Philip
→ Return journey of the Ethiopian eunuch

Joppa, where Peter raised Dorcas, is modern Jaffa, now engulfed by Tel Aviv.

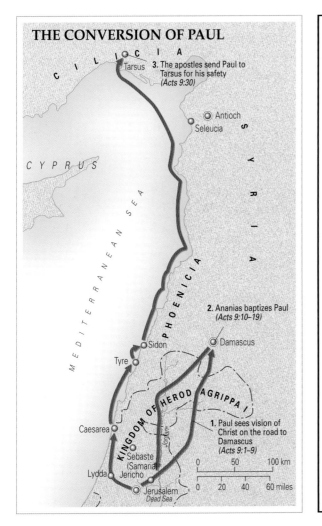

THE CONVERSION OF PAUL

3. The apostles send Paul to Tarsus for his safety (Acts 9:30)

2. Ananias baptizes Paul (Acts 9:10–19)

1. Paul sees vision of Christ on the road to Damascus (Acts 9:1–9)

CILICIA — Tarsus

CYPRUS

SYRIA — Antioch, Seleucia

MEDITERRANEAN SEA

PHOENICIA — Sidon, Tyre

Damascus

KINGDOM OF HEROD AGRIPPA I — Jordan

Caesarea

Sebaste (Samaria)

Lydda, Jericho

Jerusalem, Dead Sea

0   50   100 km
0   20   40   60 miles

Some important New Testament dates

c. 5 B.C.	The birth of Jesus
4	The death of Herod the Great
A.D. 30	The death, Resurrection and Ascension of Jesus
	Pentecost
c. 33	The conversion of Saul of Tarsus
44	The death of Herod Agrippa 1 (Acts 12:19–23)
c. 47,48	Paul's first missionary journey (Acts 13,14)
c. 49	The Council of Jerusalem (Acts 15)
c. 49–52	Paul's second missionary journey (Acts 15:40–18:22)
c. 52–56	Paul's third missionary journey (Acts 18:23–21:17)
c. 57	Paul's arrest in Jerusalem (Acts 21:27–23:30)
c. 57–59	Paul's imprisonment in Caesarea (Acts 23:31–26:32)
c. 60,61	Paul under house arrest in Rome (Acts 28:14–31)
c. 62–64	Paul at liberty again
64	The fire of Rome
	Nero's persecution of Christians
c. 65	The martyrdom of Paul
70	The destruction of Jerusalem by Titus
81–96	The reign of the Emperor Domitian
	Widespread persecution
c. 100	The death of the Apostle John

THE GENTILE MISSION

Saul of Tarsus is first mentioned in the Bible as the man who looked after the clothes of those who stoned Stephen. After Stephen's death, while Saul was still a Pharisee, he obtained permission from the temple authorities to go to Damascus to search for Christians (Acts 9:1–2). On the way there, he received a blinding vision of the risen Christ. After regaining his sight in Damascus, with the aid of Ananias in Straight Street, he learned that he had been called to be an Apostle to carry the Gospel to Gentiles as well as Jews (Acts 9:15). His conversion probably took place between three and five years after Jesus' Crucifixion.

Paul had to flee for his life back to Jerusalem (Acts 9:23–26). He was soon in danger again, from Hellenist Jews, and departed for his hometown of Tarsus, via Caesarea.

Peter's Mission

Cornelius, although a "God-fearer," on the fringes of the synagogue, was still a Gentile. As the result of a special vision, Peter was convinced that he should enter Cornelius's house and preach the Gospel to him, and that God made no distinction between Jews and Gentiles (Acts 10:47; 11:17; 15:7–11). This represented a great leap forward.

The First Gentile Church

Some of those who left Jerusalem after Stephen's martyrdom traveled north to Antioch, the capital of Syria, and the third most famous city in the Roman Empire. They preached to the Greeks, a great number of whom believed. The Jerusalem church sent Barnabas to Antioch, and he fetched Paul to help him. For a year they taught the converts in Antioch. Thus, in Antioch the first Gentile church was established, for the first time the disciples were called Christians, and the first missionary expedition was launched (Acts 11:19–26; 13:1–3) in about A.D. 47.

PAUL'S FIRST MISSIONARY JOURNEY

The missionaries chosen by the Antioch church were Barnabas and Paul, who then invited Mark (Barnabas's cousin) to accompany them. They sailed to Cyprus, Barnabas's home country, and then northwest to Asia Minor, landing at Perga in Pamphylia. By this time Mark had had enough and returned to Jerusalem.

The first Galatian city they visited was Antioch-in-Pisidia, where Paul preached in the synagogue and many Jews were converted. When unbelieving Jews contradicted Paul's message, he turned to the Gentiles. Driven out of the city by opponents, Paul and Barnabas moved on to Iconium, to Lystra—where pagans nearly worshiped them as gods, and Jews stoned Paul as a blasphemer—and Derbe.

Then they retraced their steps, encouraging the new converts and appointing elders to care for them. Back in Antioch they reported to the church what God had done, and especially how he had opened the faith to Gentiles (Acts 14:27). But a group of "Judaizers" now arrived in Antioch from Jerusalem, and started to teach that, unless Gentile converts were circumcised and kept the law of Moses, they could not be saved (Acts 15:1–5). Paul argued vigorously against them (Galatians 2:11–14).

PAUL'S FIRST MISSIONARY JOURNEY

3. Paul and Barnabas are mistaken for gods (Acts 14:8–13)

2. Elymas the sorcerer is blinded (Acts 13:6–12)

1. Paul and Barnabas set sail for Cyprus (Acts 13:4)

Right: **Remains of the Roman stadium at Perga in Pamphylia, where Paul landed in Asia Minor during his first missionary journey.**

Opposite: **Remains of the ancient Roman aqueduct at Antioch-in-Pisidia, a town in Asia Minor visited by Paul.**

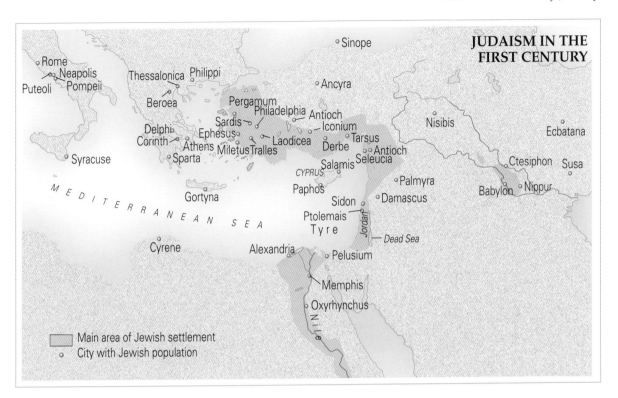

JUDAISM IN THE FIRST CENTURY

Sinope

Rome
Neapolis
Puteoli
Pompeii

Thessalonica
Philippi

Beroea

Ancyra

Pergamum
Philadelphia
Sardis
Antioch

Delphi
Corinth
Ephesus
Athens
Miletus
Tralles
Laodicea
Iconium
Tarsus
Derbe
Antioch
Seleucia

Nisibis

Ecbatana

Ctesiphon
Susa

Syracuse

Sparta

Salamis
CYPRUS

Palmyra
Babylon
Nippur

Gortyna

Paphos
Sidon
Damascus

Ptolemais
Tyre
Jordan
Dead Sea

Cyrene

Alexandria
Pelusium

Memphis

Oxyrhynchus

M E D I T E R R A N E A N   S E A

Nile

☐ Main area of Jewish settlement
○ City with Jewish population

The Antioch church now sent Paul and Barnabas to Jerusalem to attempt to settle the issue raised by the Judaizers at the Council of Jerusalem, probably in A.D. 49 or 50 (Acts 15). The Council concluded that Gentile converts did not need to be circumcised in order to be justified. Nevertheless, the Apostles asked the Gentile Christians to "remember the poor," which probably meant to take up a collection for the poorer Jerusalem Christian community, something that Paul addressed in his collections made in Gentile Christian communities.

The influence of the Judaizers on the churches of Galatia spurred Paul to write his letter to the Galatians. In it, he defended his authority as an Apostle, assured his readers there were no differences between him and the Jerusalem Apostles, rejected the Judaizers' viewpoint, stressed that one is justified by God's grace through faith alone, and begged his readers to stand fast in their Christian freedom.

83

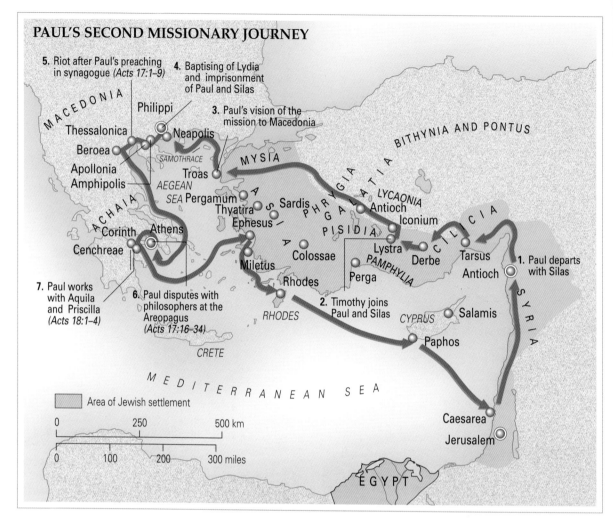

PAUL'S SECOND MISSIONARY JOURNEY

Paul next set out on his second missionary journey, accompanied by Silas. They revisited the Galatian churches, delivering the Jerusalem Council's verdict. At Lystra Paul invited the young convert Timothy to accompany them. Because Timothy had a Jewish mother, Paul even circumcised him, in deference to local Jews. Now that the principle of justification by grace alone had been established, he was prepared to make this concession (Acts 16:3; 1 Corinthians 9:19–20).

Forbidden by the Holy Spirit to travel southwest toward Ephesus or north into Bithynia, Paul and his companions instead went northwest to Troas, on the Aegean coast. Here Paul had a dream in which a Greek begged him to cross over to Macedonia and help them. Paul interpreted this as God's commission to carry the Gospel into Europe. Luke, the author of Acts, shows that he now accompanied them by using the pronoun "we" in his account for the first time.

In Macedonia, the northern province of Greece, Paul's group preached the Gospel in the three main towns: Philippi—where Paul and Silas spent a night in prison; Thessalonica—where many believed; and Berea. Women here were allowed to attend synagogue alongside the men, and so heard Paul's preaching. In Greek society women had more freedom than elsewhere and many women were baptized here.

Paul then moved on to Achaia, the southern province of Greece, visiting the two principal cities, Athens and Corinth. In Athens he preached the Gospel in the synagogue to the Jews, then in the marketplace, and finally at the famous Council of the Areopagus to its Stoic and Epicurean philosophers (Acts 17:19–34). Timothy joined him while he was in Athens, but Paul was so anxious to know how the church at Thessalonica was faring under persecution that he despatched him at once to find out (1 Thessalonians 3:1-5).

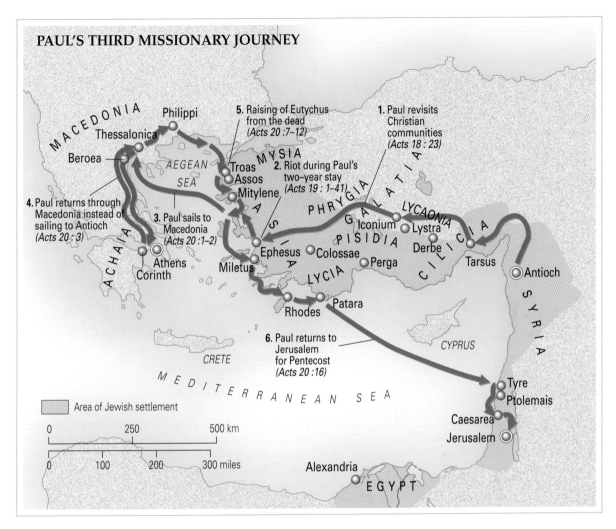

PAUL'S THIRD MISSIONARY JOURNEY

5. Raising of Eutychus from the dead (Acts 20 : 7–12)

1. Paul revisits Christian communities (Acts 18 : 23)

2. Riot during Paul's two-year stay (Acts 19 : 1–41)

4. Paul returns through Macedonia instead of sailing to Antioch (Acts 20 : 3)

3. Paul sails to Macedonia (Acts 20 : 1–2)

6. Paul returns to Jerusalem for Pentecost (Acts 20 : 16)

MACEDONIA
Philippi
Thessalonica
Beroea
AEGEAN SEA
Troas
Assos
Mitylene
MYSIA
PHRYGIA
GALATIA
LYCAONIA
Iconium
Lystra
PISIDIA
Derbe
CILICIA
Tarsus
ACHAIA
Athens
Corinth
Ephesus
Colossae
Miletus
Perga
LYCIA
Antioch
SYRIA
Rhodes
Patara
CRETE
CYPRUS
MEDITERRANEAN SEA
Tyre
Ptolemais
Caesarea
Jerusalem
Alexandria
EGYPT

Area of Jewish settlement

0   250   500 km

0   100   200   300 miles

By the time Timothy returned, Paul had moved on to Corinth (1 Thessalonians 3:6; Acts 18:5), where he founded the church that was to cause him much trouble. The encouraging news that Timothy brought prompted Paul's first letter to the Thessalonians, with the second letter following shortly after. In these letters, Paul rejoices in the Thessalonians' faith, love, and steadfastness (1 Thessalonians 1).

Paul stayed in Corinth for almost two years, following his normal practice of witnessing to the Jews first, and winning a noteworthy convert in the ruler of the synagogue, Crispus. But when the Jews opposed him, he once more turned to the Gentiles. The pro-consul of Achaia, Gallio, refused to condemn Paul, for he considered the whole affair to be a religious matter.

PAUL'S THIRD MISSIONARY JOURNEY

Paul now sailed back to Antioch, breaking his voyage with a flying visit to Ephesus, the principal city of the Roman province of Asia. The Apostle seems to have been so impressed with its importance that he went almost straight back there at the start of his third missionary journey. On this visit, after three months of preaching in the synagogue, he hired the hall of Tyrannus—presumably a secular school or lecture room—and argued the Gospel there daily for two years (Acts 19:8–10), building an important Christian church in the city (Acts 19). Christianity now spread out across western Asia Minor, reaching such towns as Colossae and Laodicea.

While Paul was in Ephesus, the church at Corinth was giving him great cause for concern. His first letter to them has been lost (1 Corinthians 5:9), although many scholars believe that a fragment of that letter is found in 2 Corinthians 6:14—7:1. However, on receiving disappointing news from Corinth, Paul wrote them a second letter, which is our 1 Corinthians. In this letter, he deplored the factions into

The great amphitheater at Ephesus, site of the riot of Ephesian silversmiths.

which the church had split (1 Corinthians 1:10–17). Paul was also horrified by the immorality and litigiousness of the church members (1 Corinthians 5–6), and by irregularities in their worship practice (1 Corinthians 11). In answer to queries, Paul also wrote about Christian marriage.

This letter evidently failed to have its intended effect, so Paul decided to visit Corinth personally. He later referred to this as a painful visit (2 Corinthians 2:1), because one of the church leaders apparently defied him publicly. So serious was this challenge that, after he left, Paul wrote the Corinthian church yet another letter, insisting that the offender be punished. This letter might be found in 2 Corinthians 10—13. At all events, this severe letter was evidently heeded and the offender duly disciplined. Paul was overjoyed to hear from Titus of the Corinthian believers' loyalty (2 Corinthians 7:12–14) and immediately wrote to them again.

In this letter, our 2 Corinthians, Paul begged them to forgive the rebel, who had received enough punishment (2 Corinthians 2:5–11), and he explained the appeal he had launched to the churches of Macedonia and Achaia to raise money for the impoverished church of Judea (2 Corinthians 8–9).

Ephesus boasted a famous temple to the goddess Artemis (Diana), one of the seven wonders of the world. As the number of converts from idolatry grew, the Ephesian silversmiths saw a threat to their sale of shrines of the goddess (Acts 19:23–41). A serious riot ensued, as a result of which Paul left the city first for Macedonia and then Achaia (Acts 19:21–22; 20:1–2).

It appears that Paul then stayed about three months in Corinth in the home of Gaius, from where he wrote the letter to the Romans (Romans 16:23; 1 Corinthians 1:14), in which he told believers in Rome how anxious he was to visit them, preach the Gospel in the imperial capital (Romans 1:8–15), and then travel on to Spain (Romans 15:18–29). He also took the opportunity to expound the Gospel at length.

After leaving Corinth, Paul and his companions began their long journey back to Jerusalem (Acts 20:3–21:16), taking with them the collection for the Judean church. They called at Troas, where Paul's sermon lasted till midnight, and Miletus, where Paul gave a moving address to the elders of the church at Ephesus.

PAUL'S ARREST AND JOURNEY TO ROME

When finally they reached their destination, Paul and his companions had not been in Jerusalem a week before some Asian Jews alleged that Paul had undermined Moses' law by his teaching and had defiled the temple by bringing in Gentiles. A riot broke out within the temple courts, and Paul was rescued from lynching by the intervention of the Roman military tribune (Acts 21:17–22:29).

Paul was now held prisoner for more than two years, and underwent a series of trials in Jerusalem

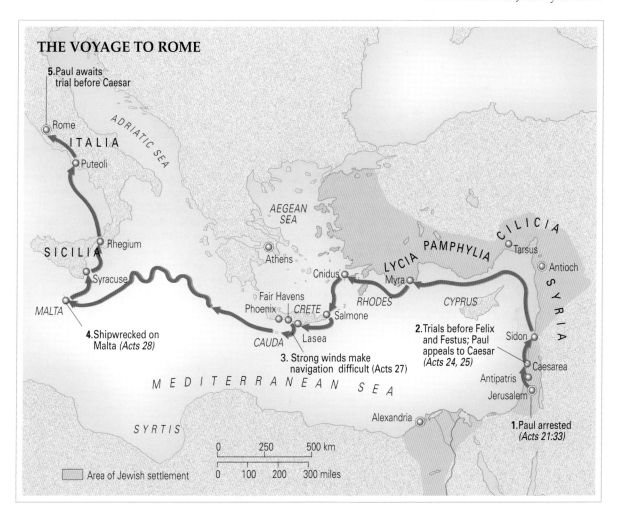

THE VOYAGE TO ROME

5. Paul awaits trial before Caesar

Rome

ITALIA

ADRIATIC SEA

Puteoli

AEGEAN SEA

Rhegium

SICILIA

Athens

Cnidus

CILICIA

PAMPHYLIA

Tarsus

LYCIA

Antioch

Myra

SYRIA

Syracuse

Fair Havens

RHODES

CYPRUS

MALTA

Phoenix | CRETE

Salmone

2. Trials before Felix and Festus; Paul appeals to Caesar (Acts 24, 25)

Sidon

4. Shipwrecked on Malta (Acts 28)

CAUDA

Lasea

Caesarea

Antipatris

3. Strong winds make navigation difficult (Acts 27)

Jerusalem

MEDITERRANEAN SEA

SYRTIS

Alexandria

1. Paul arrested (Acts 21:33)

0   250   500 km

0   100   200   300 miles

Area of Jewish settlement

and Caesarea before the Sanhedrin, the Roman procurator Felix, his successor Festus, and before King Agrippa and his wife, Bernice (Acts 22:30–23:10; 24:1–21; 25:1–26:32). However, the Apostle exercised his right as a Roman citizen to appeal to Caesar, and was finally sent to Rome for trial.

The ensuing lengthy and perilous voyage included an escape from shipwreck on the island of Malta (Acts 27:1–28:10), but at last Paul reached Rome. The believers in Rome welcomed him, and Jews came to hear the Gospel (Acts 28:30–31). The Apostle used his two years' imprisonment in Rome to write to various churches. The so-called "prison letters" belonging to

this period include Ephesians (probably a circular letter to Asian churches of the region), Colossians, Philemon (a personal letter instructing Philemon to receive back as a Christian brother his runaway slave), and Philippians. (Some scholars believe that Ephesians and Colossians were not actually written by Paul but were attributed to him by a later author.)

It is believed that Paul was released after a first trial. He might have completed his intended trip to Spain.

THE DEATHS OF PETER AND PAUL

At some point, Paul was rearrested, possibly in Spain. This time his imprisonment in Rome was not the relative freedom of a house arrest, but probably a dungeon. Paul's second letter to Timothy is placed in this period.

In this letter, he begs Timothy to visit him soon, certainly before the winter ruled out such a voyage. Now at last Paul could write: "I have fought the good fight; I have finished the race, I have kept the faith" (2 Timothy 4:7). Tradition has it that Paul was beheaded, as a Roman citizen, on the Ostian Way outside Rome, probably as part of the persecution that broke out in Rome in A.D. 64, when Nero tried to deflect responsibility for the great fire on to the Christians. (There also are serious questions about the authorship of the Pastoral Epistles: 1 and 2 Timothy and Titus.)

This same persecution forms the background to the first letter of Peter. He wrote it from Rome and addressed it to Christians in the northern parts of Asia Minor, to whom he believed persecution was shortly to come. Peter soon had to put his own instruction into practice, for he too was executed during the Neronian persecution, according to tradition being crucified upside down for he did not consider himself to be worthy to die as his Lord had died.

THE CHURCH IN ASIA MINOR

Asia Minor, with its large settled Jewish population, became the area of greatest growth for the church, as Hellenistic Jews converted to Christianity. Many of the cities with large Jewish communities now had churches.

Because of his faithful Christian witness, John the Divine was exiled to the little island of Patmos, off the west coast of Asia Minor, where he received his apocalyptic Revelation. In it, seven churches received messages both of encouragement and of condemnation (Revelation 1–3). These churches were all situated in western Asia Minor. The background to the Book of Revelation is probably the severe and widespread persecution initiated by the Emperor Domitian (A.D. 81–96).

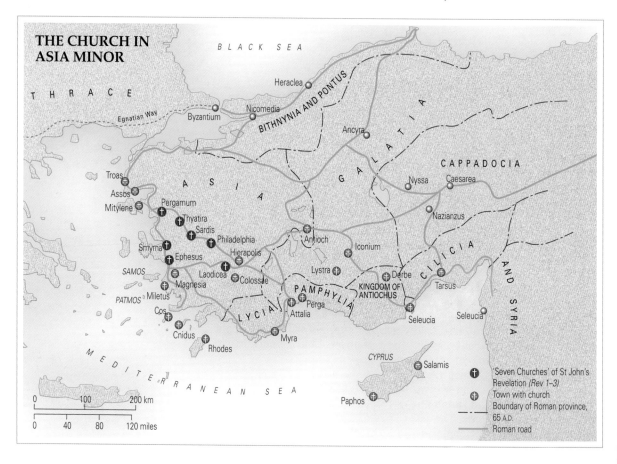

THE CHURCH IN ASIA MINOR

'Seven Churches' of St John's Revelation (Rev 1-3)
Town with church
Boundary of Roman province, 65 A.D.
Roman road

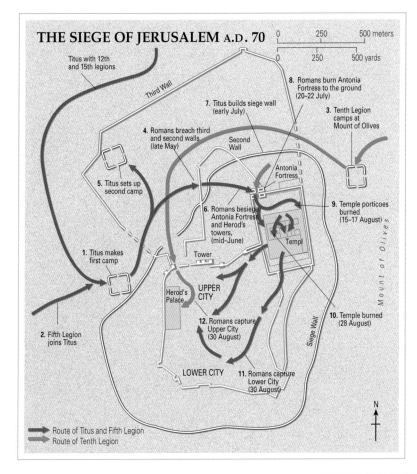

THE SIEGE OF JERUSALEM A.D. 70

0 — 250 — 500 meters
0 — 250 — 500 yards

Titus with 12th and 15th legions

Third Wall

8. Romans burn Antonia Fortress to the ground (20–22 July)

7. Titus builds siege wall (early July)

3. Tenth Legion camps at Mount of Olives

4. Romans breach third and second walls (late May)

Second Wall

5. Titus sets up second camp

Antonia Fortress

6. Romans besiege Antonia Fortress and Herod's towers, (mid–June)

9. Temple porticoes burned (15–17 August)

Temple

1. Titus makes first camp

Tower

Herod's Palace

UPPER CITY

12. Romans capture Upper City (30 August)

Mount of Olives

10. Temple burned (28 August)

2. Fifth Legion joins Titus

Siege Wall

LOWER CITY

11. Romans capture Lower City (30 August)

N

Route of Titus and Fifth Legion
Route of Tenth Legion

The Fall of Masada

Masada is a massive outcrop of rock in the Judean Desert, which the Hasmoneans had fortified. Herod the Great built a palace complex on the summit. After the fall of Jerusalem, a Zealot group under Eleazar took refuge there. With plenty of food and water, they were able to withstand the Roman offensive until A.D. 73.

The Romans first built a siege wall around the rock to prevent the supply of more rations. They then built an earth ramp up the west side of the rock. On this ramp, a base of wood and iron supported a siege tower. The Romans then had a vantage point from which to breach with a battering ram the main wall surrounding the summit of the rock. Realizing their hopeless plight, it appears that 960 Jews committed suicide overnight, while awaiting the final assault. To this day Masada is a symbol of Jewish resistance to tyranny.

THE FIRST JEWISH REVOLT

From A.D. 44, Judea was under the control of Roman procurators. Since the days of Herod the Great, the Zealot party had been in revolt against Rome. Now, with increasing intolerance toward the Jews and the desecration of the temple by the Emperor Caligula, the Roman authorities provoked the Pharisees into joining ranks with the Zealots.

Once the revolt had sparked, it spread quickly through most of Judea and Galilee. The Roman general Vespasian arrived in Caesarea and set up his base at Ptolemais. He rapidly recaptured Galilee and the Golan in A.D. 67, before turning south. Despite the Jews' common hatred of the Romans, the war occasioned a good deal of factional fighting that the Romans were able to exploit. The Jews' lack of unity resulted in the relentless reoccupation by the Romans of Samaria, Peraea, and Judea.

In spite of fierce defense by the Zealots, Titus, Vespasian's son, did not take long to capture Jerusalem, building a siege wall to starve out its inhabitants. Within three months of the beginning of the siege, the temple had been burned and the other buildings destroyed.

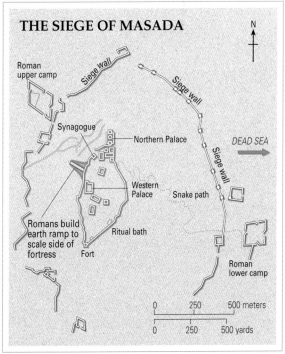

THE SIEGE OF MASADA

N

Roman upper camp

Siege wall

Siege wall

Synagogue

Northern Palace

DEAD SEA

Siege wall

Western Palace

Snake path

Romans build earth ramp to scale side of fortress

Ritual bath

Fort

Roman lower camp

0 — 250 — 500 meters
0 — 250 — 500 yards

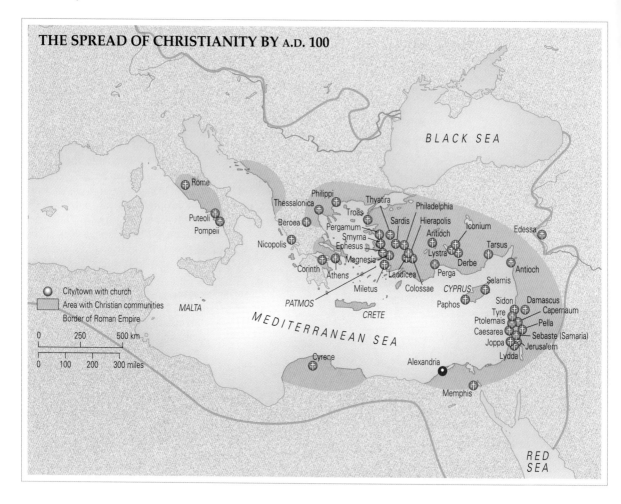

THE SPREAD OF CHRISTIANITY BY A.D. 100

Legend:
- City/town with church
- Area with Christian communities
- Border of Roman Empire

0   250   500 km

0   100   200   300 miles

BLACK SEA

MEDITERRANEAN SEA

RED SEA

Rome, Puteoli, Pompeii, Nicopolis, Beroea, Thessalonica, Philippi, Troas, Pergamum, Smyrna, Ephesus, Magnesia, Corinth, Athens, Miletus, PATMOS, MALTA, CRETE, Cyrene, Alexandria, Memphis, Thyatira, Sardis, Philadelphia, Hierapolis, Laodicea, Colossae, Antioch, Lystra, Perga, Derbe, Iconium, Tarsus, CYPRUS, Paphos, Salamis, Edessa, Antioch, Sidon, Tyre, Ptolemais, Caesarea, Joppa, Lydda, Damascus, Capernaum, Pella, Sebaste (Samaria), Jerusalem

THE THIRD JEWISH REVOLT

After the disastrous Jewish War (A.D. 66–73) and the harsh suppression of a further Jewish revolt during the reign of the Emperor Trajan, many Jews fled to the safety of the Babylonian community, which lay outside the Roman Empire. However, there remained a current of sedition that surfaced again in the person of Simon bar Kosiba.

Bar Kosiba was hailed as the Messiah, and in a reference to Numbers 24:17 he was also known as bar Kochba, "son of the star." With widespread support, though not that of the Jewish Christian population, who obviously did not consider him the Messiah, a well-planned revolt led to the immediate evacuation of Jerusalem by the Romans.

Judea was largely governed by the Jews until A.D. 133, when Rome gradually reasserted control. Village after village was destroyed in the merciless suppression, until bar Kochba himself was killed in the last stronghold at Bethar. Some of his supporters fled to caves in the hills beside the Dead Sea, but without ultimate escape.

Roman authorities destroyed all Jewish and Christian shrines in the land. They then planted sacred groves over the ruins to desecrate them. This made it easier for St. Helena, the mother of Emperor Constantine, to find Christian sites in the early 4th century A.D. She only had to look for the groves in a relatively treeless environment.

THE SPREAD OF CHRISTIANITY BY A.D. 100

As we have seen, Paul and his fellow Jewish Apostles carried the Gospel to regions beyond this area. With the express purpose of evangelizing the Gentiles, they traveled extensively in Asia Minor and Greece. They visited synagogues in the Jewish Diaspora and talked with Gentiles in the marketplaces. Behind them they left small, uncertain groups of Christians whose faith was nurtured in subsequent visits and in the letters we know from the New Testament.

By the end of the first century, Christianity was more or less confined to the eastern Roman Empire, except for communities in Rome, Puteoli, and around the Bay

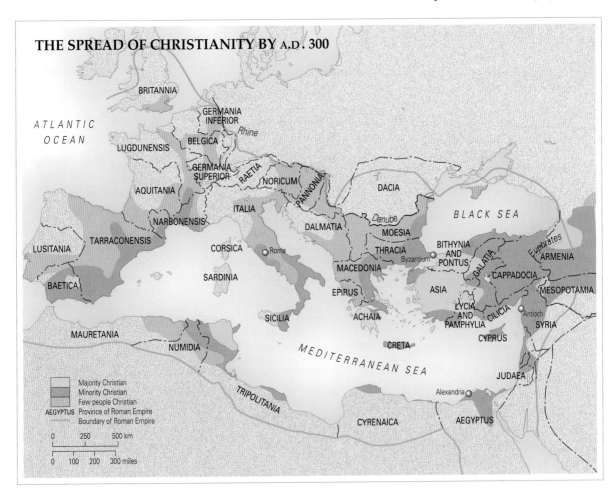

THE SPREAD OF CHRISTIANITY BY A.D. 300

Legend:
- Majority Christian
- Minority Christian
- Few people Christian
- AEGYPTUS Province of Roman Empire
- Boundary of Roman Empire

0   250   500 km

0   100   200   300 miles

of Naples. The only possible church known outside the empire was at Edessa. Names of cities with Christians are known from the New Testament, such as the seven churches of Revelation, and from contemporary correspondence. The early Christian writer Ignatius tells of churches in Magnesia and Tralles, and later writers of a church in Alexandria, the home of Paul's helper Apollos.

THE SPREAD OF CHRISTIANITY BY A.D. 300

By the end of the third century, the Christian world looked quite different. In the changes following the failure of the Jewish revolts, the Church and Judaism had increasingly gone their separate ways.

Christianity now became largely a religion of the Gentiles. With the expansion of the Church westward as far as Roman Britain, its informal center shifted from Jerusalem to Rome. The scene was now set for Emperor Constantine to embrace Christianity c. A.D. 312. By the end of the fourth century Christianity would be the official religion of the empire.

Index of Place Names

General Index